THIS IS YOUR **PASSBOOK**® FOR ...

DENTAL ASSISTING

NATIONAL LEARNING CORPORATION®
passbooks.com

COPYRIGHT NOTICE

Copyright © 2020 by

N L C ®

National Learning Corporation

212 Michael Drive, Syosset, NY 11791
(516) 921-8888 • www.passbooks.com
E-mail: info@passbooks.com

PUBLISHED IN THE UNITED STATES OF AMERICA

PASSBOOK® SERIES

THE *PASSBOOK® SERIES* has been created to prepare applicants and candidates for the ultimate academic battlefield – the examination room.

At some time in our lives, each and every one of us may be required to take an examination – for validation, matriculation, admission, qualification, registration, certification, or licensure.

Based on the assumption that every applicant or candidate has met the basic formal educational standards, has taken the required number of courses, and read the necessary texts, the *PASSBOOK® SERIES* furnishes the one special preparation which may assure passing with confidence, instead of failing with insecurity. Examination questions – together with answers – are furnished as the basic vehicle for study so that the mysteries of the examination and its compounding difficulties may be eliminated or diminished by a sure method.

This book is meant to help you pass your examination provided that you qualify and are serious in your objective.

The entire field is reviewed through the huge store of content information which is succinctly presented through a provocative and challenging approach – the question-and-answer method.

A climate of success is established by furnishing the correct answers at the end of each test.

You soon learn to recognize types of questions, forms of questions, and patterns of questioning. You may even begin to anticipate expected outcomes.

You perceive that many questions are repeated or adapted so that you can gain acute insights, which may enable you to score many sure points.

You learn how to confront new questions, or types of questions, and to attack them confidently and work out the correct answers.

You note objectives and emphases, and recognize pitfalls and dangers, so that you may make positive educational adjustments.

Moreover, you are kept fully informed in relation to new concepts, methods, practices, and directions in the field.

You discover that you arre actually taking the examination all the time: you are preparing for the examination by "taking" an examination, not by reading extraneous and/or supererogatory textbooks.

In short, this PASSBOOK®, used directedly, should be an important factor in helping you to pass your test.

OCCUPATIONAL COMPETENCY EXAMINATIONS (OCE)

GENERAL

The Occupational Competency Examinations are intended for those individuals experienced in skilled trades or occupations who need to present objective evidence of their competency to become vocational teachers, to obtain academic credit from a higher institution, or to secure teacher certification.

In addition to meeting university admission requirements for fully matriculated students -- and for teacher certification -successful completion of the exam provides opportunity to earn up to 36 semester hours of collegiate credit for applied occupational skills and technical knowledge. The credit may be used toward advanced study and degrees in occupational education in several states.

NATURE OF THE EXAMINATION

The examination consists of two parts -- Written and Performance. The written test covers factual knowledge, technical information, understanding of principles and problem solving abilities related to the occupation. The performance test is designed to sample the manipulative skills required by an occupation. Thus it enables the candidate to demonstrate that he possesses the knowledge and skills that a competent craftsman employs in his daily work.

ADVANTAGES

The Prospective Teacher - Tradesmen and other technically competent persons who wish to enter industrial education training programs.

Industrial Teacher Educators - The OCE Tests provide the industrial teacher educator with an objective and dependable means for assessing the trade competency of applicants for admission to their programs.

Certifying Agencies - The OCE Tests provide an objective method for assessing occupational competence in qualifying for certification.

Directors of Vocational Education Programs - The OCE Tests provide a recruitment and selection procedure that is reliable, objective and fair to all recipients

Candidates for Academic Degrees - The OCE Tests are accepted by many colleges and universities for granting of credit or advanced standing for occupational experience.

PLACE OF EXAMINATION

A network of 36 Area Test Centers has been established throughout the United States in the States listed below. Tests are generally conducted twice a year at these centers, as well as other locations, depending on need.

Alabama	Kentucky	Oregon
Arkansas	Massachusetts	Pennsylvania
California	Michigan	South Dakota
Colorado	Missouri	Tennessee
Connecticut	Montana	Texas
Florida	Nebraska	Utah
Georgia	New Jersey	Vermont
Hawaii	New York	Virginia
Idaho	North Dakota	Washington
Illinois	Ohio	West Virginia
Iowa	Oklahoma	Wisconsin

OCE TESTS OFFERED

Interested candidates are alerted to the occupations listed below as scheduled for examination. Individuals should notify the NOCTI if they wish to be examined in an occupation not listed.

Air Conditioning and Refrigeration
Airframe or Power plant Mechanics
Appliance Repair
Architectural Drafting
Auto Body Repair
Automatic Heating
Auto Mechanics
Building Maintenance
Cabinetmaking and Millwork
Carpentry
Commercial and Advertising Art
Commercial Photography
Cosmetology
Data Processing
Dental Assisting
Diesel Engine Repair
Dressmaking

Electrical Installation
Electronics Communication
General Printing Industrial Electronics
Machine Trades
Masonry
Machine Drafting
Mechanical Technology
Medical Assisting Offset Lithography
Ornamental Horticulture
Plumbing
Quantity Food Preparation
Sheet Metal Fabrication
Small Engine Repair
Welding

HOW TO REGISTER

For registration information contact Educational Testing Service of Princeton, New Jersey.

Dental Assistant

BACKGROUND

The training of dental assistants in colleges and technical schools is a recent development. In the past, a dental assistant received on-the-job training from her employer. Dependence on such training, however, does not meet modern needs. Not only is it too slow and uncertain, but many dentists do not train their assistants beyond routine duties. As a result many dental assistants today are not utilized to their full potential.

Recent studies show that by using an assistant effectively in a two-chair office a dentist can almost double the number of his patients. A trained assistant can demonstrate her economic value from the very outset of her employment.

The urgency for trained dental assistants stems from the shortage of dentists (1 dentist for every 2,100 persons). Not only is the population and the demand for dental service growing far more rapidly than dentists are being trained, but a larger percentage of the total population is seeking dental service today than ever before. To meet adequately the needs for the future, dental colleges would have to begin now to double the number they graduate annually. By increasing the efficiency and quantity of service provided by the dentist, the trained assistant can aid in alleviating the current shortage of dental manpower.

NATURE OF WORK

A trained dental assistant divides her work between (1) assisting in treatment duties and (2) office management. Her primary function is assisting at the chairside where she plays an active and integral role in dental procedures. For example, she prepares patients for treatment, sets out instruments in the order they are to be used, checks equipment, sterilizes instruments, keeps an inventory of all materials used, and orders new supplies as needed. She does laboratory work, such as making study models of teeth and casting inlays, thus relieving the dentist of much time consuming work. Her duties include exposing and processing of X-rays and mounting of the radiographs in the proper holder.

During treatment she keeps the operating field clear, mixes filling materials and dental cements and passes these materials and instruments to the dentist as he needs them.

As office manager, she acts as receptionist, schedules appointments, keeps accounts and records, sends out bills and is responsible for the general appearance of the office.

NUMBER OF WORKERS ENGAGED

The American Dental Association reports that nonsalaried dentists employed about 270,000 full- and part-time dental assistants.

According to "The Survey of Dentistry," about 90 percent of the dental assistants in the country were employed by two-thirds of the private dentists. The remainder worked in hospitals of the Public Health Service and the Veterans Administration, in local public health departments or private clinics, or in the armed services.

Most currently employed dental assistants are trained on-the-job. While the number of formal training programs is rapidly increasing, only a small fraction of dental assistants have had technical college or college training. (This is not the case with dental hygienists who complete a basic 2-year collegiate program and are licensed to practice by State dental boards. The primary duties of hygienist are cleaning teeth and instructing patients in oral hygiene practices.)

DISTRIBUTION

The demand for dental assistants in any specific area is dependent on the number of dentists in that area.

TRENDS AND OUTLOOKS

The demand for trained dental assistants is greater than the supply. The growing shortage of dentists coupled with the increasing demand for dental service is making the need for assistants more acute.

Dental colleges are teaching their students how to use trained dental assistants effectively. Most young dentists entering practice are eager to secure the service of an assistant who has had technical chairside training.

Also, dentists with an established practice are discovering the economic advantage of employing a trained assistant.

AGE

Dental assistants may be anywhere from 18 to more than 60 years old.

PHYSICAL, MENTAL, PERSONALITY QUALIFICATIONS

A pleasant personality is essential in dealing with the dentist's patients. The assistant should be neat, clean, and healthy, have poise and self-control.

She should have more than average intelligence, be able to meet people and put them at ease. She should have a good command of the language and be able to express herself clearly and pleasantly.

Naturally, ability to work quickly and deftly with her hands is extremely important for effective performance at the chairside and in the laboratory.

GENERAL EDUCATION

A young woman planning to become a trained dental assistant will find that a general business program in high school will equip her for the office management duties. Courses in mathematics, bookkeeping, and typing will be particularly useful. If biology and chemistry courses can be included in her curriculum, they will also be helpful.

TRAINING CENTERS

Many dental colleges, junior colleges, and vocational schools now offer courses in dental assisting with their number expected to increase rapidly over the next several years.

Junior colleges offer 1- and 2-year courses, the latter giving the prospective assistant both a broad academic foundation as well as specialized training in dental assisting. Some of the junior colleges award an associate arts degree upon completion of the 2-year program. Courses of 1 year or less concentrate on the more technical aspects of dental assisting.

METHODS OF ENTERING OCCUPATION

Schools and colleges offering courses in dental assisting have a placement service and ordinarily there is no difficulty in placing graduates in acceptable jobs. The American Dental Association is also active in placing qualified assistants.

State and private employment agencies provide channels for placing the trained assistant. Family dentists, the local dental assistant association, the local dental society, and dental schools can offer helpful suggestions about employment opportunities.

EARNINGS

A dental assistant's salary range is dependent on several factors. Amount of special school or college training, length of practical experience, and geographic location must all be considered in determining salaries.

PENSIONS

There is no organized pension system for dental assistants. A dental assistant can obtain coverage under social security, but unless she works in an office that is subject to State unemployment tax, she cannot draw unemployment benefits.

NONMONETARY REWARDS

A dental assistant derives prestige and satisfaction from the semi-professional status of her work and her association with professional people. Furthermore, as a member of a health team she is making a real contribution to the health and well-being of the individual and the community.

HOW TO TAKE A TEST

You have studied long, hard and conscientiously.

With your official admission card in hand, and your heart pounding, you have been admitted to the examination room.

You note that there are several hundred other applicants in the examination room waiting to take the same test.

They all appear to be equally well prepared.

You know that nothing but your best effort will suffice. The "moment of truth" is at hand: you now have to demonstrate objectively, in writing, your knowledge of content and your understanding of subject matter.

You are fighting the most important battle of your life—to pass and/or score high on an examination which will determine your career and provide the economic basis for your livelihood.

What extra, special things should you know and should you do in taking the examination?

I. YOU MUST PASS AN EXAMINATION

A. WHAT EVERY CANDIDATE SHOULD KNOW
Examination applicants often ask us for help in preparing for the written test. What can I study in advance? What kinds of questions will be asked? How will the test be given? How will the papers be graded?

B. HOW ARE EXAMS DEVELOPED?
Examinations are carefully written by trained technicians who are specialists in the field known as "psychological measurement," in consultation with recognized authorities in the field of work that the test will cover. These experts recommend the subject matter areas or skills to be tested; only those knowledges or skills important to your success on the job are included. The most reliable books and source materials available are used as references. Together, the experts and technicians judge the difficulty level of the questions.

Test technicians know how to phrase questions so that the problem is clearly stated. Their ethics do not permit "trick" or "catch" questions. Questions may have been tried out on sample groups, or subjected to statistical analysis, to determine their usefulness.

Written tests are often used in combination with performance tests, ratings of training and experience, and oral interviews. All of these measures combine to form the best-known means of finding the right person for the right job.

II. HOW TO PASS THE WRITTEN TEST

A. BASIC STEPS

1) Study the announcement

How, then, can you know what subjects to study? Our best answer is: "Learn as much as possible about the class of positions for which you've applied." The exam will test the knowledge, skills and abilities needed to do the work.

Your most valuable source of information about the position you want is the official exam announcement. This announcement lists the training and experience qualifications. Check these standards and apply only if you come reasonably close to meeting them. Many jurisdictions preview the written test in the exam announcement by including a section called "Knowledge and Abilities Required," "Scope of the Examination," or some similar heading. Here you will find out specifically what fields will be tested.

2) Choose appropriate study materials

If the position for which you are applying is technical or advanced, you will read more advanced, specialized material. If you are already familiar with the basic principles of your field, elementary textbooks would waste your time. Concentrate on advanced textbooks and technical periodicals. Think through the concepts and review difficult problems in your field.

These are all general sources. You can get more ideas on your own initiative, following these leads. For example, training manuals and publications of the government agency which employs workers in your field can be useful, particularly for technical and professional positions. A letter or visit to the government department involved may result in more specific study suggestions, and certainly will provide you with a more definite idea of the exact nature of the position you are seeking.

3) Study this book!

III. KINDS OF TESTS

Tests are used for purposes other than measuring knowledge and ability to perform specified duties. For some positions, it is equally important to test ability to make adjustments to new situations or to profit from training. In others, basic mental abilities not dependent on information are essential. Questions which test these things may not appear as pertinent to the duties of the position as those which test for knowledge and information. Yet they are often highly important parts of a fair examination. For very general questions, it is almost impossible to help you direct your study efforts. What we can do is to point out some of the more common of these general abilities needed in public service positions and describe some typical questions.

1) General information

Broad, general information has been found useful for predicting job success in some kinds of work. This is tested in a variety of ways, from vocabulary lists to questions about current events. Basic background in some field of work, such as sociology or economics, may be sampled in a group of questions. Often these are principles which have become familiar to most persons through exposure rather than through formal training. It is difficult to advise you how to study for these questions; being alert to the world around you is our best suggestion.

2) Verbal ability

An example of an ability needed in many positions is verbal or language ability. Verbal ability is, in brief, the ability to use and understand words. Vocabulary and grammar tests are typical measures of this ability. Reading comprehension or paragraph interpretation questions are common in many kinds of civil service tests. You are given a paragraph of written material and asked to find its central meaning.

IV. KINDS OF QUESTIONS

1. Multiple-choice Questions

Most popular of the short-answer questions is the "multiple choice" or "best answer" question. It can be used, for example, to test for factual knowledge, ability to solve problems or judgment in meeting situations found at work.

A multiple-choice question is normally one of three types:
- It can begin with an incomplete statement followed by several possible endings. You are to find the one ending which *best* completes the statement, although some of the others may not be entirely wrong.
- It can also be a complete statement in the form of a question which is answered by choosing one of the statements listed.
- It can be in the form of a problem – again you select the best answer.

Here is an example of a multiple-choice question with a discussion which should give you some clues as to the method for choosing the right answer:

When an employee has a complaint about his assignment, the action which will *best* help him overcome his difficulty is to
   A. discuss his difficulty with his coworkers
   B. take the problem to the head of the organization
   C. take the problem to the person who gave him the assignment
   D. say nothing to anyone about his complaint

In answering this question, you should study each of the choices to find which is best. Consider choice "A" – Certainly an employee may discuss his complaint with fellow employees, but no change or improvement can result, and the complaint remains unresolved. Choice "B" is a poor choice since the head of the organization probably does not know what assignment you have been given, and taking your problem to him is known as "going over the head" of the supervisor. The supervisor, or person who made the assignment, is the person who can clarify it or correct any injustice. Choice "C" is, therefore, correct. To say nothing, as in choice "D," is unwise. Supervisors have and interest in knowing the problems employees are facing, and the employee is seeking a solution to his problem.

2. True/False

3. Matching Questions
Matching an answer from a column of choices within another column.

V. RECORDING YOUR ANSWERS

Computer terminals are used more and more today for many different kinds of exams.

For an examination with very few applicants, you may be told to record your answers in the test booklet itself. Separate answer sheets are much more common. If this separate answer sheet is to be scored by machine – and this is often the case – it is highly important that you mark your answers correctly in order to get credit.

VI. BEFORE THE TEST

YOUR PHYSICAL CONDITION IS IMPORTANT
If you are not well, you can't do your best work on tests. If you are half asleep, you can't do your best either. Here are some tips:

1) Get about the same amount of sleep you usually get. Don't stay up all night before the test, either partying or worrying—DON'T DO IT!
2) If you wear glasses, be sure to wear them when you go to take the test. This goes for hearing aids, too.
3) If you have any physical problems that may keep you from doing your best, be sure to tell the person giving the test. If you are sick or in poor health, you relay cannot do your best on any test. You can always come back and take the test some other time.

Common sense will help you find procedures to follow to get ready for an examination. Too many of us, however, overlook these sensible measures. Indeed, nervousness and fatigue have been found to be the most serious reasons why applicants fail to do their best on civil service tests. Here is a list of reminders:

• Begin your preparation early – Don't wait until the last minute to go scurrying around for books and materials or to find out what the position is all about.
• Prepare continuously – An hour a night for a week is better than an all-night cram session. This has been definitely established. What is more, a night a week for a month will return better dividends than crowding your study into a shorter period of time.
• Locate the place of the exam – You have been sent a notice telling you when and where to report for the examination. If the location is in a different town or otherwise unfamiliar to you, it would be well to inquire the best route and learn something about the building.
• Relax the night before the test – Allow your mind to rest. Do not study at all that night. Plan some mild recreation or diversion; then go to bed early and get a good night's sleep.
• Get up early enough to make a leisurely trip to the place for the test – This way unforeseen events, traffic snarls, unfamiliar buildings, etc. will not upset you.

- Dress comfortably – A written test is not a fashion show. You will be known by number and not by name, so wear something comfortable.
- Leave excess paraphernalia at home – Shopping bags and odd bundles will get in your way. You need bring only the items mentioned in the official notice you received; usually everything you need is provided. Do not bring reference books to the exam. They will only confuse those last minutes and be taken away from you when in the test room.
- Arrive somewhat ahead of time – If because of transportation schedules you must get there very early, bring a newspaper or magazine to take your mind off yourself while waiting.
- Locate the examination room – When you have found the proper room, you will be directed to the seat or part of the room where you will sit. Sometimes you are given a sheet of instructions to read while you are waiting. Do not fill out any forms until you are told to do so; just read them and be prepared.
- Relax and prepare to listen to the instructions
- If you have any physical problem that may keep you from doing your best, be sure to tell the test administrator. If you are sick or in poor health, you really cannot do your best on the exam. You can come back and take the test some other time.

VII. AT THE TEST

The day of the test is here and you have the test booklet in your hand. The temptation to get going is very strong. Caution! There is more to success than knowing the right answers. You must know how to identify your papers and understand variations in the type of short-answer question used in this particular examination. Follow these suggestions for maximum results from your efforts:

1) Cooperate with the monitor
The test administrator has a duty to create a situation in which you can be as much at ease as possible. He will give instructions, tell you when to begin, check to see that you are marking your answer sheet correctly, and so on. He is not there to guard you, although he will see that your competitors do not take unfair advantage. He wants to help you do your best.

2) Listen to all instructions
Don't jump the gun! Wait until you understand all directions. In most civil service tests you get more time than you need to answer the questions. So don't be in a hurry. Read each word of instructions until you clearly understand the meaning. Study the examples, listen to all announcements and follow directions. Ask questions if you do not understand what to do.

3) Identify your papers
Civil service exams are usually identified by number only. You will be assigned a number; you must not put your name on your test papers. Be sure to copy your number correctly. Since more than one exam may be given, copy your exact examination title.

4) Plan your time
Unless you are told that a test is a "speed" or "rate of work" test, speed itself is usually not important. Time enough to answer all the questions will be provided, but this

does not mean that you have all day. An overall time limit has been set. Divide the total time (in minutes) by the number of questions to determine the approximate time you have for each question.

5) Do not linger over difficult questions

If you come across a difficult question, mark it with a paper clip (useful to have along) and come back to it when you have been through the booklet. One caution if you do this – be sure to skip a number on your answer sheet as well. Check often to be sure that you have not lost your place and that you are marking in the row numbered the same as the question you are answering.

6) Read the questions

Be sure you know what the question asks! Many capable people are unsuccessful because they failed to *read* the questions correctly.

7) Answer all questions

Unless you have been instructed that a penalty will be deducted for incorrect answers, it is better to guess than to omit a question.

8) Speed tests

It is often better NOT to guess on speed tests. It has been found that on timed tests people are tempted to spend the last few seconds before time is called in marking answers at random – without even reading them – in the hope of picking up a few extra points. To discourage this practice, the instructions may warn you that your score will be "corrected" for guessing. That is, a penalty will be applied. The incorrect answers will be deducted from the correct ones, or some other penalty formula will be used.

9) Review your answers

If you finish before time is called, go back to the questions you guessed or omitted to give them further thought. Review other answers if you have time.

10) Return your test materials

If you are ready to leave before others have finished or time is called, take ALL your materials to the monitor and leave quietly. Never take any test material with you. The monitor can discover whose papers are not complete, and taking a test booklet may be grounds for disqualification.

VIII. EXAMINATION TECHNIQUES

1) Read the general instructions carefully. These are usually printed on the first page of the exam booklet. As a rule, these instructions refer to the timing of the examination; the fact that you should not start work until the signal and must stop work at a signal, etc. If there are any *special* instructions, such as a choice of questions to be answered, make sure that you note this instruction carefully.

2) When you are ready to start work on the examination, that is as soon as the signal has been given, read the instructions to each question booklet, underline any key words or phrases, such as *least, best, outline, describe*

and the like. In this way you will tend to answer as requested rather than discover on reviewing your paper that you *listed without describing*, that you selected the *worst* choice rather than the *best* choice, etc.

3) If the examination is of the objective or multiple-choice type – that is, each question will also give a series of possible answers: A, B, C or D, and you are called upon to select the best answer and write the letter next to that answer on your answer paper – it is advisable to start answering each question in turn. There may be anywhere from 50 to 100 such questions in the three or four hours allotted and you can see how much time would be taken if you read through all the questions before beginning to answer any. Furthermore, if you come across a question or group of questions which you know would be difficult to answer, it would undoubtedly affect your handling of all the other questions.

4) If the examination is of the essay type and contains but a few questions, it is a moot point as to whether you should read all the questions before starting to answer any one. Of course, if you are given a choice – say five out of seven and the like – then it is essential to read all the questions so you can eliminate the two that are most difficult. If, however, you are asked to answer all the questions, there may be danger in trying to answer the easiest one first because you may find that you will spend too much time on it. The best technique is to answer the first question, then proceed to the second, etc.

5) Time your answers. Before the exam begins, write down the time it started, then add the time allowed for the examination and write down the time it must be completed, then divide the time available somewhat as follows:
   - If 3-1/2 hours are allowed, that would be 210 minutes. If you have 80 objective-type questions, that would be an average of 2-1/2 minutes per question. Allow yourself no more than 2 minutes per question, or a total of 160 minutes, which will permit about 50 minutes to review.
   - If for the time allotment of 210 minutes there are 7 essay questions to answer, that would average about 30 minutes a question. Give yourself only 25 minutes per question so that you have about 35 minutes to review.

6) The most important instruction is to *read each question* and make sure you know what is wanted. The second most important instruction is to *time yourself properly* so that you answer every question. The third most important instruction is to *answer every question*. Guess if you have to but include something for each question. Remember that you will receive no credit for a blank and will probably receive some credit if you write something in answer to an essay question. If you guess a letter – say "B" for a multiple-choice question – you may have guessed right. If you leave a blank as an answer to a multiple-choice question, the examiners may respect your feelings but it will not add a point to your score. Some exams may penalize you for wrong answers, so in such cases *only*, you may not want to guess unless you have some basis for your answer.

7) Suggestions
  a. Objective-type questions
    1. Examine the question booklet for proper sequence of pages and questions
    2. Read all instructions carefully
    3. Skip any question which seems too difficult; return to it after all other questions have been answered
    4. Apportion your time properly; do not spend too much time on any single question or group of questions
    5. Note and underline key words – *all, most, fewest, least, best, worst, same, opposite,* etc.
    6. Pay particular attention to negatives
    7. Note unusual option, e.g., unduly long, short, complex, different or similar in content to the body of the question
    8. Observe the use of "hedging" words – *probably, may, most likely,* etc.
    9. Make sure that your answer is put next to the same number as the question
    10. Do not second-guess unless you have good reason to believe the second answer is definitely more correct
    11. Cross out original answer if you decide another answer is more accurate; do not erase until you are ready to hand your paper in
    12. Answer all questions; guess unless instructed otherwise
    13. Leave time for review

  b. Essay questions
    1. Read each question carefully
    2. Determine exactly what is wanted. Underline key words or phrases.
    3. Decide on outline or paragraph answer
    4. Include many different points and elements unless asked to develop any one or two points or elements
    5. Show impartiality by giving pros and cons unless directed to select one side only
    6. Make and write down any assumptions you find necessary to answer the questions
    7. Watch your English, grammar, punctuation and choice of words
    8. Time your answers; don't crowd material

8) Answering the essay question

Most essay questions can be answered by framing the specific response around several key words or ideas. Here are a few such key words or ideas:

M's: manpower, materials, methods, money, management
P's: purpose, program, policy, plan, procedure, practice, problems, pitfalls, personnel, public relations
  a. Six basic steps in handling problems:
    1. Preliminary plan and background development
    2. Collect information, data and facts
    3. Analyze and interpret information, data and facts
    4. Analyze and develop solutions as well as make recommendations

5. Prepare report and sell recommendations
6. Install recommendations and follow up effectiveness

b. Pitfalls to avoid
1. *Taking things for granted* – A statement of the situation does not necessarily imply that each of the elements is necessarily true; for example, a complaint may be invalid and biased so that all that can be taken for granted is that a complaint has been registered
2. *Considering only one side of a situation* – Wherever possible, indicate several alternatives and then point out the reasons you selected the best one
3. *Failing to indicate follow up* – Whenever your answer indicates action on your part, make certain that you will take proper follow-up action to see how successful your recommendations, procedures or actions turn out to be
4. *Taking too long in answering any single question* – Remember to time your answers properly

EXAMINATION SECTION

EXAMINATION SECTION
TEST 1

DIRECTIONS: Each question or incomplete statement is followed by several suggested answers or completions. Select the one that BEST answers the question or completes the statement. *PRINT THE LETTER OF THE CORRECT ANSWER IN THE SPACE AT THE RIGHT.*

1. It is IMPORTANT to be familiar with dental terminology so that you can   1.____

    A. tell the patients why certain instruments are used
    B. do your work more efficiently
    C. let the patients see that you know what you are doing
    D. know what supplies to order for the clinic

2. Assume that you do not remember when the dentist told you to make the next appoint-   2.____
ment for a particular patient.
The BEST course of action for you to take is to

    A. use your own judgment and give the patient an appointment
    B. check with the dentist
    C. let the patient decide when he wants to come
    D. give the patient the next free appointment

3. Assume that in the process of putting away some dental instruments, you find that one,   3.____
which is not used frequently, is rusty.
Of the following, the BEST action for you to take is to

    A. throw the instrument away and order another in its place
    B. put the instrument in a sterilizer
    C. leave the instrument alone since it is not frequently used
    D. show the instrument to the dentist and ask what you should do

4. A child of four years of age, on his first visit to the dental clinic in which you are employed,   4.____
refuses to enter the dentist's room to undergo treatment, shows fear, and creates a small
disturbance in the outer office.
The MOST acceptable course of action for you to follow is to

    A. do nothing
    B. offer the child anything he wants in order to appease him
    C. tell the child how important dental care is
    D. allow the child to watch another child during treatment who has willingly submitted
thereto

5. Assume that the mother of one of the children who has had a tooth extracted at the clinic   5.____
on the previous day telephones to say that the child's gum bled all night. You should

    A. tell her to apply a warm application
    B. tell her that you will inform the dentist and call her back
    C. ask her what she has done for the child
    D. tell her not to bring the child to the clinic

6. Assume that the dentist who is assigned to the clinic telephones to state that he will be about an hour late on arriving at the clinic.
The one of the following which is the BEST action for you to take is to

    A. say nothing to the patients
    B. telephone the patients who have later appointments and tell them not to come
    C. ask the patients who arrived for the early appointments to come back
    D. ask all patients if they can wait; if not, give them another appointment

6.___

7. A patient under care at the clinic enters the clinic and shows an irritable and demanding manner in requesting to see the dentist immediately.
The MOST acceptable course of conduct for you to follow is to

    A. inform the dentist of the patient's presence immediately so that he can explain the circumstances to the patient himself
    B. explain to the patient that the dentist is busy and request him to be seated
    C. give the patient a sedative and ask him to rest on the office couch until he is in a calmer mood
    D. maintain a firm position in refusing to allow him to see the dentist and request the patient to leave the office

7.___

8. To discuss the history or treatment of a patient with another patient is

    A. *inadvisable* because it might tend to lessen the confidence of the patient in the skills of the dentist
    B. *advisable* because it will stimulate an interest in the patient concerning the progress of her own treatment
    C. *inadvisable* because such information must always be treated as confidential
    D. *advisable* because it will place the patient at ease and aid the dentist in preparing her for treatment

8.___

9. The branch of dentistry CHIEFLY concerned with the correction of irregular teeth is known as

    A. prosthodontia   B. peridontia
    C. orthodontia   D. oxodontia

9.___

10. The dentist stated that the patient was suffering from a severely impacted tooth.
The word *impacted* means MOST NEARLY the

    A. most severe stage of dental caries
    B. inability of a tooth to erupt properly
    C. condition of defective nerve tissues within the tooth
    D. improper insertion of a gold inlay

10.___

11. In dentistry, a retractor is used CHIEFLY to

    A. draw back the cheeks of a patient to allow the dentist more working space
    B. withdraw instrument trays from the sterilizer
    C. regulate the amount of anesthetic distributed by the inhalation machine
    D. regulate the speed of the drill attached to the dental unit

11.___

12. The instrument MOST commonly used to administer a local anesthesia is a   12.____

    A. forceps   B. die
    C. syringe   D. contra-angle

13. An obstreperous patient is one who is   13.____

    A. cooperative   B. quiet and reserved
    C. frightened   D. noisy and unruly

14. Of the following, the LEAST essential in arranging a tray for cavity preparation and fillings is   14.____

    A. a scaler   B. a bur
    C. a forceps   D. novocaine

15. The etiology of a dental defect refers to the _____ the defect.   15.____

    A. cause of   B. stage of
    C. correction of   D. damaged caused by

Questions 16-25.

DIRECTIONS: Column I lists words connected with the practice of dentistry. Column II lists words and phrases which best describe or define or are closely related to the words listed in Column I. In the space at the right, opposite the numbers 16 through 25, place the letter preceding the word or phrase in Column II which BEST describes or defines, or is most closely related to, the word listed in Column I.

COLUMN I	COLUMN II	
16. Amalgam	A. used in temporary fillings	16.____
17. Ampoule	B. anesthetic	17.____
18. Autoclave	C. hermetically sealed vial	18.____
19. Gutta-percha	D. cleansing agent	19.____
20. Mandible	E. alloy of mercury	20.____
21. Maxilla	F. sterilization of instruments	21.____
22. Porcelain	G. standard dental unit	22.____
23. Procaine	H. lower jaw	23.____
24. Detergent	I. ingredient used in making alloys	24.____
25. Cassette	J. upper jaw	25.____
	K. solution used in x-ray development	
	L. holds x-ray films	

KEY (CORRECT ANSWERS)

1.	B		11.	A
2.	B		12.	C
3.	D		13.	D
4.	D		14.	C
5.	B		15.	A
6.	D		16.	E
7.	B		17.	C
8.	C		18.	F
9.	C		19.	A
10.	B		20.	H

21.	J
22.	I
23.	B
24.	D
25.	L

___

TEST 2

DIRECTIONS: Each question or incomplete statement is followed by several suggested answers or completions. Select the one that BEST answers the question or completes the statement. *PRINT THE LETTER OF THE CORRECT ANSWER IN THE SPACE AT THE RIGHT.*

1. When referring to the teeth, cervix means MOST NEARLY the

   A. root   B. crown   C. neck   D. pulp

   1.____

2. The part of the x-ray machine which automatically controls the length of time for an exposure is called a

   A. volt-meter   B. time switch
   C. milliammeter   D. safety valve

   2.____

3. An anodyne is BEST defined as a(n)

   A. pain reliever
   B. part of an electric transformer
   C. antiseptic
   D. part of an x-ray tube

   3.____

4. Deciduous teeth are also known as

   A. permanent teeth   B. molars
   C. baby teeth   D. diseased teeth

   4.____

5. The substance MOST commonly used for protection against x-ray radiation is

   A. zinc   B. steel   C. lead   D. porcelain

   5.____

6. The developer for the x-ray reproductions should ALWAYS be kept at a temperature of APPROXIMATELY

   A. 50-60° F   B. 65-75° F   C. 80-90° F   D. 95-105° F

   6.____

7. Scaling and curetting of teeth are MOST closely associated with

   A. prophylaxis   B. extraction of teeth
   C. filling of cavities   D. oral surgery

   7.____

8. Of the following pieces of equipment, the one which is NOT a part of the standard dental unit is the

   A. cuspidor   B. bracket table
   C. articulator   D. electric cautery

   8.____

9. Spatula is BEST defined as a(n)

   A. soluble substance used in the preparation of amalgams
   B. knife-shaped instrument used in mixing plasters and cements
   C. solution used in the development of x-ray films
   D. instrument used in dental surgery

   9.____

10. Trench mouth is the COMMONLY known term for

    A. Rigg's Disease   B. nephritis
    C. Vincent's Disease   D. yellow jaundice

    10.____

11. The substance USUALLY used to make positive impressions of the mouth is   11._____

    A.   cement
    B.   putty
    C.   plaster of Paris
    D.   clay compound

12. The terms *visual method* and *time temperature method* refer to   12._____

    A.   x-ray film development
    B.   the administration of an anesthesia
    C.   oral surgery
    D.   sterilization procedures

13. Roentgenology is CHIEFLY concerned with the study of   13._____

    A.   dental diseases
    B.   x-ray films
    C.   mechanical disorders of the mouth
    D.   operative dentistry

14. Dental tape is used for   14._____

    A.   prophylactic treatment
    B.   sealing dental records
    C.   administering a local anesthesia
    D.   measuring the dentition of a patient

Questions 15-20.

DIRECTIONS: Below is a diagram of a permanent upper palate. For Questions 15 through 20, print in the space at the right alongside each of the numbers 15 through 20 the capital letter which on the diagram represents the tooth named in that question.

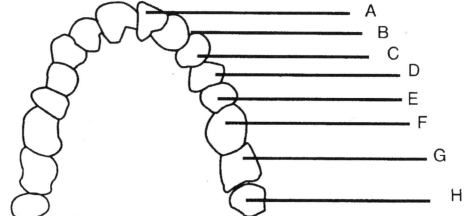

15. First bicuspid   15._____

16. First molar   16._____

17. Wisdom tooth   17._____

18. Second molar   18._____

19. Lateral incisor   19._____

20. Eye tooth   20._____

KEY (CORRECT ANSWERS)

1.	C	11.	C
2.	B	12.	A
3.	A	13.	B
4.	C	14.	A
5.	C	15.	D
6.	B	16.	F
7.	A	17.	H
8.	C	18.	G
9.	B	19.	B
10.	C	20.	C

———

EXAMINATION SECTION
TEST 1

DIRECTIONS: Each question or incomplete statement is followed by several suggested answers or completions. Select the one that BEST answers the question or completes the statement. *PRINT THE LETTER OF THE CORRECT ANSWER IN THE SPACE AT THE RIGHT.*

1. The PRINCIPAL hand instruments used for cavity preparation are

1.____

    A. chisels and excavators   B. burs and centra-angles
    C. forceps and elevators   D. mallets and articulators

2. A mandrel is a(n)

2.____

    A. surgical instrument used in the extraction of teeth
    B. shaft which fits into the handpiece of a dental engine
    C. small bowl in which substances may be crushed or ground
    D. instrument used in the dental laboratory to represent a combination of the upper and lower dentitions

3. Of the following dental defects, the one which is HOT considered a form of malocclusion is

3.____

    A. malposition of the teeth   B. excessive overbite
    C. diseased teeth   D. excessive underbite

4. Prosthetic dentistry is CHIEFLY concerned with

4.____

    A. preventive procedures
    B. scientific research to determine the causes of various dental disorders
    C. oral surgery
    D. providing artificial substitutes for missing teeth

5. Of the following, the one which is NOT an anesthetic is

5.____

    A. ethyl chloride   B. procaine
    C. novocaine   D. sodium chloride

6. A fissure is a(n)

6.____

    A. instrument used for exploring cavities
    B. opening in the bone permitting the passage of nerves and blood vessels
    C. groove in the enamel of the teeth
    D. tough fibrous band which connects bones and muscles

7. A pedodontist is a dentist who specializes in

7.____

    A. root canal therapy   B. child dentistry
    C. operative dentistry   D. preventive dentistry

8. The concentration of fluorine in water is known to have a GREAT effect in

8.____

    A. reducing the appearance of dental caries
    B. increasing the susceptibility to pyorrhea
    C. reducing the appearance of hypoplasia
    D. increasing the susceptibility to dental trauma

9. The element of the tooth which imparts color and bulk to the tooth is the   9.____

   A. enamel   B. cementum   C. dentine   D. pulp

10. When filing record cards of patients in alphabetical order, the one of the following names   10.____
which should be filed THIRD is

   A. Wyndam   B. Wynant   C. Winston   D. Winsten

11. When filing record cards of patients in alphabetical order, the one of the following names   11.____
which should be filed FOURTH is

   A. Smith   B. Smithe   C. Smythe   D. Smutz

12. When filing record cards of patients in alphabetical order, the one of the following names   12.____
which should be filed SECOND is

   A. Thatcher   B. Thackerey   C. Thaddeus   D. Thaoker

13. When filing record cards of patients in alphabetical order, the one of the following names   13.____
which should be filed SECOND is

   A. Johnson   B. Johnston   C. Johansen   D. Johnstown

14. When filing record cards of patients in alphabetical order, the one of the following names   14.____
which should be filed FIRST is

   A. Mullaney   B. Mulreney   C. Mulligan   D. Mullins

Questions 15-20.

DIRECTIONS: Questions 15 through 20 are to be answered on the basis of the chart given below.

MONTHLY REPORT OF X CLINIC APRIL							
				SALARIES			
	Patients Registered	Patients Treated	Laundry Expenses	Hygienists	Dentists	Dental Assts.	Materials-
Week 1	465	205	$348.60	$680.00	$1200.00	$480.00	$159.00
Week 2	535	225	369.00	880.00	1972.00	720.00	568.80
Week 3	204	202	183.20	740.00	1600.00	600.00	574.32
Week 4	427	217	278.88	856.00	1540.00	740.00	210.28

15. The total expenses for Week 3 EXCEED the total expenses for Week 1 by   15.____

   A. $817.92   B. $819.12   C. $829.92   D. $833.88

16. The percentage of all registered patients who were actually treated during the four weeks   16.____
of April is MOST NEARLY

   A. 19%   B. 49%   C. 52%   D. 90%

17. The expenses for materials for the four weeks of April EXCEED the expenses for laundry for the same four-week period by 17.____

    A. $325.52   B. $328.72   C. $332.72   D. $353.24

18. Considering only the expenses listed on the monthly report, the average cost per patient treated during Week 4 is MOST NEARLY 18.____

    A. $12.68   B. $16.72   C. $20.00   D. $24.76

19. If the clinic remained open for five full days each week, with three dentists on duty at all times, the AVERAGE number of patients treated per day by each dentist during Week 2 would be 19.____

    A. 6   B. 12   C. 15   D. 18

20. The TOTAL amount spent for hygienists' salaries for the four-week period is 20.____

    A. 75% of the total salaries paid to dentists during the four-week period
    B. equal to the total expenses for Week 1
    C. less than the total salaries paid to the dental assistants for the four-week period
    D. 50% of the total salaries paid to dentists for the four-week period

---

KEY (CORRECT ANSWERS)

1.	A	11.	C
2.	B	12.	D
3.	C	13.	A
4.	D	14.	A
5.	D	15.	C
6.	C	16.	C
7.	B	17.	C
8.	A	18.	B
9.	C	19.	C
10.	B	20.	D

TEST 2

1. An adult's dentition usually consists of thirty-two permanent teeth.

    1._____

2. When taking x-ray pictures, it is advisable for the dentist or his assistant to hold the film packet in place during the operation of the machine.

    2._____

3. Before placing the x-ray film in the hypo-solution, it must be placed in the developing solution.

    3._____

4. Drying of x-ray films may be hastened by the use of an electric fan without inflicting any blemish or injury upon the film.

    4._____

5. X-ray machines can operate only on direct current.

    5._____

6. Nitrous oxide is a safe anesthesia to administer to children.

    6._____

7. The MOST efficient method of sterilizing cutting instruments in order to prevent dulling the cutting edges is to immerse them in boiling water.

    7._____

8. A peroxide solution is often used in curing halitosis.

    8._____

9. Mastication is the first step in the digestive process.

    9._____

10. A superficial examination is one which is thorough and complete.

    10._____

11. When a person brushes his teeth more than once daily, it is GENERALLY advisable to use a different toothbrush each time.

    11._____

12. A mortar and pestle are used in the trituration of dental substances.

    12._____

13. In x-ray work, it is considered good practice to allow an old x-ray to remain on the machine after one has finished using it.

    13._____

14. Memory may be safely relied upon in keeping track of important papers taken from the file.

    14._____

15. To file letters or other papers in order by their dates is to file them in numerical order.

    15._____

16. A pending file is one which contains all matters which have been disposed of permanently.

    16._____

17. A synonym for periodontitis is pyorrhea.

    17._____

18. The phrase *keystone of the dental arch* refers to the six-year molars.

    18._____

19. A proficient dental assistant is one who is not suited for his work.

    19._____

20. If a visitor were to faint in the office, it would be advisable for the dental assistant to keep the head of the visitor lower than is feet.

    20._____

21. The duties of a dental hygienist and those of a dental assistant are identical.   21.____

22. Third molars are sometimes referred to as wisdom teeth.   22.____

23. There are usually twenty-four teeth in the normal dentition of a three-year-old child.   23.____

24. A bur is an instrument used to prepare cavities for filling.   24.____

25. Dental caries may be defined as tooth decay.   25.____

26. A stimulator is used to activate the gingival tissues in order to make them resistant to   26.____
     infections and mechanical disorders.

27. Resuscitation is a method of administering local anesthesia to a patient.   27.____

28. An opaque object is transparent.   28.____

29. The duties of a dental assistant usually include administering anesthesia to patients.   29.____

30. The duties of a dental assistant usually include spanking an unruly child in the reception   30.____
     room.

———

KEY (CORRECT ANSWERS)

1.	T	16.	F
2.	F	17.	T
3.	T	18.	T
4.	T	19.	F
5.	F	20.	T
6.	T	21.	F
7.	F	22.	T
8.	T	23.	F
9.	T	24.	T
10.	F	25.	T
11.	T	26.	T
12.	T	27.	F
13.	T	28.	F
14.	F	29.	F
15.	F	30.	F

———

EXAMINATION SECTION
TEST 1

DIRECTIONS: Each question or incomplete statement is followed by several suggested answers or completions. Select the one that BEST answers the question or completes the statement. *PRINT THE LETTER OF THE CORRECT ANSWER IN THE SPACE AT THE RIGHT.*

1. Oral hygiene has as its CHIEF object the

   A. curing of dental caries
   B. replacement of lost teeth
   C. prevention of dental diseases
   D. establishing of a training program for dentists

1.____

2. The one of the following which is NOT properly a function of the dental assistant is to

   A. sterilize and clean the dental engine
   B. clean and polish the teeth of school children
   C. mix silicates and other materials
   D. introduce new patients to the dentist

2.____

3. If a dental assistant is called upon to do all of the following at the same time, she should FIRST

   A. answer the telephone
   B. clean the dental bracket
   C. give the patient who is about to leave another appointment
   D. receive patients just arrived

3.____

4. Assume that you accidentally destroy a memorandum containing information relating to a telephone call you received for the dentist. You don't remember the message accurately. It would be MOST advisable for you to

   A. forget the incident; the man will probably call again
   B. explain the situation to the dentist when he arrives
   C. check the red book under *dentists;* this should give you a clue since the caller was probably an associate
   D. write another memorandum including what you believe to be the correct information; the dentist will be able to detect any discrepancies

4.____

5. A patient wishes to make another appointment at a time which is already filled. After you inform her of this, she asks to see the appointment book so that she may determine the opening most convenient for her.
   As dental assistant, you should

   A. show her the book and let her choose the most convenient time
   B. refer the request to the dentist and await his direction
   C. explain politely that all office records are confidential and try to give her another convenient appointment
   D. give her the appointment for the period originally requested and make the required adjustment later

5.____

6. The one of the following which is NOT among the duties expected of a dental assistant during the process of tooth removal is

    6.____

    A. having the patient's x-ray films in readiness
    B. sterilizing all instruments to be used
    C. sponging and swabbing in order to maintain a clear operating field
    D. incising the gum in order to expose the bone, in cases of impaction

7. Assume that, as dental assistant, you ruin a whole series of radiograms.
You should

    7.____

    A. destroy the films and all notations relating to them since disclosure of the incident may mean losing your job
    B. call the situation to the attention of the dentist
    C. call the patient for another appointment in order to take a new set of radiograms
    D. replace them with a similar set of films of the patient's mouth taken a year ago

8. For a dental assistant to greet patients by name is

    8.____

    A. *advisable;* such greeting creates a friendly atmosphere
    B. *inadvisable;* familiarity breeds contempt
    C. *advisable;* the patient is thus assured that the assistant is competent
    D. *inadvisable;* the assistant cannot remember the names of all the patients and all should be treated alike

9. Assume that you receive a telephone call for Dr. Angell, your employer, who is busy with a patient.
The MOST acceptable procedure for you to follow generally is to

    9.____

    A. call, *Dr. Angell, you're wanted on the telephone*
    B. tell the caller that the dentist is not in and take a message
    C. give the dentist a written message and await his reply
    D. tell the caller that the dentist is busy and take a message

10. Of the following, the information LEAST essential on a patient's personal record card is the

    10.____

    A. work done at each sitting
    B. dentist's findings at the first examination
    C. home address and telephone number of the patient
    D. time the patient entered and left the operating room

11. Assume that a patient requiring immediate attention arrives while others are waiting to be treated by the dentist.
The dental assistant should

    11.____

    A. ask the patient to await his turn since rules must be uniformly applied
    B. immediately usher the patient into the operating room for emergency treatment
    C. explain the situation to the dentist and await his direction
    D. inform the patient that the dentist may be busy for some time and suggest that he try to get dental treatment elsewhere

12. For the dental assistant to attempt to interest the child patient in some toy or book during his first visit before the dentist is ready for the appointment is

   12._____

   A. *advisable;* this will relieve the parent of the care of the child
   B. *inadvisable;* the spirit of play thus created will make him more difficult to handle in the dentist chair
   C. *advisable;* this procedure will help make him feel more at home with his surroundings
   D. *inadvisable;* she can utilize her time more effectively by performing other functions

13. A dental assistant may be required to use the *tickler system* in connection with her work. This system refers to a

   13._____

   A. method of artificial respiration
   B. clerical procedure commonly used for the periodic recall of patients
   C. continuous inventory of all supplies on hand
   D. bookkeeping system generally employed for recording the outlay of petty cash

14. When arranging the record cards of patients in alphabetical order, the one of the following names which should be filed THIRD is

   14._____

   A. James S. Dougerty   B. J.P. Doyle
   C. Joseph A. Dougherty   D. Jas. S. Dugan

15. The one of the following names which should be filed SECOND is

   15._____

   A. G.E. Jones   B. George E. Johnson
   C. Edward G. Jonson   D. E. George Jonus

16. The one of the following names which should be filed LAST is

   16._____

   A. Albert J. Thomas   B. J.A. Tenneson
   C. John J. Tomlinson   D. James Thompson

17. Of the following, the one which is NOT generally a symptom of shock is

   17._____

   A. cold sweat
   B. a flushed face
   C. nausea
   D. an anxious, frightened expression

18. To reduce swelling and relieve pain following the extraction of a number of teeth, the patient should be advised to apply

   18._____

   A. a hot compress
   B. a medicated poultice
   C. alternating hot and cold compresses
   D. an ice pack

19. A patient who is usually very nervous and worried about pain faints in the waiting room. The dentist has not yet arrived.
Of the following, the BEST procedure for the dental assistant to follow is to

   19._____

   A. slap the patient's face in order to revive her
   B. lower her head and hold smelling salts close to her nose until she comes to
   C. carry her to a couch and keep her covered until she recovers
   D. call an ambulance at once as she may be seriously ill

20. A patient suffering from hemophilia requires special attention if the dentist is going to　　20.____

    A. fill a tooth　　　　　　　　　　　　B. set a crown
    C. extract a tooth　　　　　　　　　　D. make a denture

21. Children should generally begin their FIRST visit to the dentist at about the age of　　21.____
    _____ years.

    A. 3　　　　　　B. 6　　　　　　C. 10　　　　　　D. 12

22. Deciduous teeth are _____ teeth.　　22.____

    A. artificial　　　　　　　　　　　　B. grinding
    C. permanent　　　　　　　　　　　D. milk

23. The FIRST set of human teeth usually contains _____ teeth.　　23.____

    A. 16　　　　　　B. 20　　　　　　C. 24　　　　　　D. 32

24. The teeth known as *premolars* are the　　24.____

    A. bicuspids　　　　　　　　　　　　B. first molars
    C. cuspids　　　　　　　　　　　　　D. incisors

25. The wisdom teeth are also known as　　25.____

    A. tearing teeth　　　　　　　　　　B. third molars
    C. second molars　　　　　　　　　D. temporary teeth

KEY (CORRECT ANSWERS)

1.	C		11.	C
2.	B		12.	C
3.	A		13.	B
4.	B		14.	B
5.	C		15.	A
6.	D		16.	C
7.	B		17.	B
8.	A		18.	D
9.	D		19.	B
10.	D		20.	C

21.	A
22.	D
23.	B
24.	A
25.	B

TEST 2

DIRECTIONS: Each question or incomplete statement is followed by several suggested answers or completions. Select the one that BEST answers the question or completes the statement. *PRINT THE LETTER OF THE CORRECT ANSWER IN THE SPACE AT THE RIGHT.*

1. The FIRST permanent tooth usually erupts at about the age of _____ years.   1.____

   A. four   B. six   C. eight   D. ten

2. The expression *eye tooth* refers to the   2.____

   A. upper canines   B. upper premolars
   C. lower incisors   D. lower bicuspids

3. The FIRST permanent molar displaces   3.____

   A. the first deciduous molar   B. the second deciduous molar
   C. the deciduous cuspid   D. none of the deciduous teeth

4. The bulk of the hard structure of the tooth is formed of   4.____

   A. dentin   B. enamel   C. cementum   D. pulp

5. The *pulp* of the tooth is commonly called the   5.____

   A. root   B. neck   C. nerve   D. crown

6. The one of the following which is LEAST essential in arranging the tray for an extraction is   6.____

   A. novacaine   B. forceps   C. pumice   D. gauze

7. The one of the following which is LEAST essential in arranging the tray for prophylactic treatment is   7.____

   A. an explorer   B. disclosing solution
   C. rubber dam   D. cotton pliers

8. Of the following, the one which is LEAST essential in arranging the tray for an amalgam filling is a(n)   8.____

   A. mouth mirror   B. bur
   C. explorer   D. sprue

9. When the dentist speaks of the *cementum,* he is referring to the   9.____

   A. material used for filling teeth permanently
   B. tissue forming the body of the tooth
   C. material used for filling teeth temporarily
   D. tissue which covers the root portion of the tooth

10. An *elevator* is an instrument MOST commonly used to   10.____

   A. remove tooth roots
   B. clean and polish the roots of teeth
   C. remove caries from a cavity in a tooth
   D. clean the root canal of a tooth

11. When the dentist asks his assistant for the *matrix*, the assistant knows that the dentist is planning to   11.___

    A. shell off the tooth enamel
    B. prepare the stump of a tooth for a crown
    C. pack amalgam into a cavity
    D. treat gum tissue

12. The one of the following which is NOT a significant reason for keeping *stones* wet during their use in cavity preparation is that   12.___

    A. this procedure helps their smooth action
    B. this helps to preserve the stones
    C. the likelihood of pain is thus lessened
    D. such action assures continued sterility of the stones

13. A dental assistant should know that when the dentist calls for an *excavator*, he is MOST probably going to   13.___

    A. prepare the tooth for extraction
    B. remove deposits from the teeth
    C. prepare a tooth cavity
    D. adjust the patient's bite

14. *Scalers* and *curets* are GENERALLY used to   14.___

    A. give the patient a prophylaxis
    B. prepare the patient's tooth for a cavity
    C. examine for caries
    D. perform root canal work

15. Water used for spraying a cavity should   15.___

    A. be hot   B. approximate body temperature
    C. be cool   D. be cold

16. *Amalgam* is the material used by the dentist for   16.___

    A. filling a cavity permanently   B. filling a cavity temporarily
    C. cementing inlays   D. performing a prophylaxis

17. Of the following, the one which is used in making dental amalgams is   17.___

    A. mercury   B. gold
    C. nickel   D. plaster-of-paris

18. The material GENERALLY employed for cementing gold inlays is   18.___

    A. quicksilver   B. shellac
    C. zinc-oxyphosphate   D. calcium phosphate

19. When the dentist says that a child's teeth are going through a process of *exfoliation,* he means that they are

    A. decaying   B. becoming discolored
    C. loosening and dropping out   D. erupting

19.____

20. A dentist engaged in the treatment of diseases of the tissues surrounding the tooth is practicing

    A. oxodentia   B. prosthetics
    C. orthodentia   D. periodentia

20.____

21. The term *hypoplasia* is applied to

    A. poor structural development of tissue
    B. dental caries
    C. disintegration of teeth already formed
    D. the formation of calculus

21.____

22. The one of the following which is the MOST reliable indication of pyorrhea is

    A. pus and inflammation of the gums
    B. dark enamel
    C. notched and thin-edged incisors
    D. malocclusion of the teeth

22.____

23. The CHIEF use of alcohol in dentistry is as a(n)

    A. antiseptic   B. heart depressant
    C. anesthetic   D. sedative

23.____

24. The PRINCIPAL chemical components of a tooth are

    A. calcium and sulphur   B. calcium and phosphorus
    C. phosphorus and sulphur   D. sulphur and iron

24.____

25. Of the following conditions, the one LEAST conducive to the growth of oral bacteria is

    A. warmth
    B. light
    C. moisture
    D. an adequate supply of proper food

25.____

KEY (CORRECT ANSWERS)

1.	B		11.	C
2.	A		12.	D
3.	D		13.	C
4.	A		14.	A
5.	C		15.	B
6.	C		16.	A
7.	C		17.	A
8.	D		18.	C
9.	D		19.	C
10.	A		20.	D

21.	A
22.	A
23.	A
24.	B
25.	B

EXAMINATION SECTION
TEST 1

DIRECTIONS: Each question or incomplete statement is followed by several suggested answers or completions. Select the one that BEST answers the question or completes the statement. *PRINT THE LETTER OF THE CORRECT ANSWER IN THE SPACE AT THE RIGHT.*

1. Digestive enzymes are

    A. cells which secrete digestive juices
    B. bacteria which ferment foods
    C. secreted substances which hydrolyze food
    D. the products of digestion

1._____

2. The apparatus used by dental assistants for sterilizing dental equipment by the use of steam under pressure is called a(n)

    A. reamer   B. autoclave
    C. pyrometer   D. electroplate

2._____

3. Of the following instruments, the one which is LEAST advisable sterilized by the use of an autoclave is the

    A. explorer   B. mouth mirror
    C. cotton plier   D. scalpel

3._____

4. The BEST way to sterilize dry gauze dressings and towels is by

    A. boiling in a sterilizer for 20 minutes
    B. dipping into a sterilizing solution
    C. by an autoclave
    D. washing with a good detergent and rinsing thoroughly

4._____

5. In order to cleanse and polish a sterilizer effectively, it is MOST desirable to boil it in a solution of

    A. water and vinegar   B. water and bicarbonate of soda
    C. alcohol and formaldehyde   D. water and borax

5._____

6. The substance which would MOST appropriately be added to water to prevent dental instruments from rusting during the process of wet heat sterilization is

    A. salt   B. bicarbonate of soda
    C. copper sulphate   D. phenol

6._____

7. Of the following, the one which is LEAST properly a function of the dental assistant in dental x-ray work is

    A. mounting the films   B. making the exposure
    C. developing the films   D. giving x-ray interpretations

7._____

8. Of the following statements, the one which is LEAST accurate in connection with the process of developing x-ray films is: 8.____

   A. The only light permissible in a developing room is that furnished by a blue light
   B. Developing and fixing solutions must be fresh for best results
   C. The temperature of the developer should not be above 75° F or below 65° F
   D. The x-ray films should be rinsed after immersion in the developing solution

9. X-ray films are stored in lead containers CHIEFLY because   9.____

   A. such containers retain the temperature necessary to preserve the film
   B. they are moisture-proof
   C. such containers protect the film from exposure to stray x-rays
   D. they are dust-proof

10. In taking dental x-rays, the time necessary for each exposure is LEAST affected by the   10.____

   A. position of the tooth in the mount
   B. thickness of the bone
   C. age of the patient
   D. length of time the film was stored before usage

11. Bite-wing dental films are used MOST frequently to   11.____

   A. locate unerupted teeth
   B. test for gingivitis
   C. locate the presence of cavities
   D. detect fractures of the jaw

12. The one which is LEAST likely to cause a radiogram to appear dark is   12.____

   A. light leaks in the dark room
   B. prolonged developing
   C. old and oxidized solution
   D. too brilliant ruby light

13. The word *alloy* means MOST NEARLY   13.____

   A. anesthetic
   B. antiseptic
   C. antidote
   D. metallic mixture

14. The dentist studied the *anatomy* of the tooth. *Anatomy,* as used in this sentence, means MOST NEARLY   14.____

   A. structure
   B. fillings
   C. cavities
   D. location

15. A *chronic* condition is one that is   15.____

   A. prolonged
   B. temporary
   C. painful
   D. fundamental

16. An assistant should *anticipate* the questions of the patients. *Anticipate,* as used in this sentence, means MOST NEARLY   16.____

   A. repeat   B. encourage   C. foresee   D. present

24

17. The patient asked for a *postponement* of treatment.   17.____
    Postponement, as used in this sentence, means MOST NEARLY

    A. explanation   B. delay
    C. cancellation   D. modification

18. A dental assistant should know that the word *aseptic* means MOST NEARLY   18.____

    A. soiled   B. mouldy
    C. poisonous   D. sterile

19. An *effective* manner of speaking is one that is   19.____

    A. artificial   B. striking
    C. domineering   D. nervous

20. The expenditures for additional dental supplies were carefully *scrutinized.*   20.____
    Scrutinized, as used in this sentence, means MOST NEARLY

    A. limited   B. eliminated
    C. balanced   D. examined

21. An action which is *juvenile* is   21.____

    A. evil   B. youthful
    C. legal   D. precocious

22. To say that a man lacks *integrity* is to say that he is   22.____

    A. fearless   B. ignorant
    C. dishonest   D. unprejudiced

23. It is in the reception room that the patient first senses the atmosphere of the entire office.   23.____
    Softly shaded lamps, comfortable chairs, magazines, a few well-chosen pictures help to
    relieve the patient of the subconscious idea that he is walking into a torture chamber.
    From this statement, we may conclude MOST NEARLY that

    A. the dentist's reception room should be furnished expensively in order that the
    patient may relax comfortably
    B. all patients consider the dentist to be one who inflicts torture
    C. a pleasantly furnished reception room tends to create a favorable reaction on the
    part of the patient
    D. it is unnecessary to be concerned with the appearance of the operating room, pro-
    viding the reception room is tastefully furnished

24. Dentists have come to realize, in recent years, that care of the teeth during childhood is   24.____
    not only a valuable service in that period but plays an important part in the whole life his-
    tory of the individual.
    From this statement, we may conclude that

    A. proper care of a child's teeth will eliminate the necessity for dental care during
    adulthood
    B. dental services should commence early in the life of an individual
    C. healthy permanent teeth invariably follow healthy baby teeth
    D. early dental care will help to increase the life span of an individual

25. In well-managed offices, the assistant functions as a second brain and another pair of
hands that attend to all duties which do not actually require the knowledge, skill, and
legal right of a dentist.
From this statement, we may conclude MOST NEARLY that

    A. the dental assistant should be able to substitute for the dentist in an emergency
    B. an intelligent assistant is also a competent one
    C. every dentist should employ an assistant in order to function efficiently
    D. the dental assistant is an important member of the dental staff

Questions 26-30.

DIRECTIONS: Questions 26 through 30 are to be answered on the basis of the following
chart.

SUPPLIES USED IN XYZ CLINIC
DURING WEEK OF MAY 15

On Hand	Towels	Paper Cups	Gauze Squares	Aprons	Cotton Rolls
at Beginning of Week	678	1254	376	80	310
Used on Monday	104	62	42	12	36
Used on Tuesday	112	58	37	10	44
Used on Wednesday	115	68	52	11	38
Used on Thursday	122	63	45	14	50
Used on Friday	117	59	39	11	42

26. On the basis of the above chart, it is CORRECT to say that

    A. fewer aprons and gauze squares were used on Tuesday than on any other day
    B. although more paper cups were used on Monday, fewer towels and cotton rolls
       were used on that day than on any other day
    C. more paper cups and fewer cotton rolls were used on Wednesday than on any
       other day
    D. although more cotton rolls and towels were used on Thursday, fewer aprons were
       used on that day than on any other day

27. The average number of towels used during the week given exceeds the average number
of gauze squares used during the same period of time by

    A. 68   B. 71   C. 78   D. 81

28. Assuming that supplies were delivered semi-annually, the minimum number of paper
cups which will probably be required for the next six months, on the basis of the figures
above, is MOST NEARLY

    A. 1250   B. 2000   C. 8250   D. 16,500

29. The difference between the largest and the smallest total number of supplies used on
any day during the given week is

    A. 18   B. 27   C. 37   D. 43

30. The supply of aprons on hand at the beginning of the week has decreased, at the end of   30.____
    the week, by APPROXIMATELY

    A. 22%   B. 27%   C. 39%   D. 73%

KEY (CORRECT ANSWERS)

1.	C	16.	C
2.	B	17.	B
3.	D	18.	D
4.	C	19.	B
5.	A	20.	D
6.	B	21.	B
7.	D	22.	C
8.	A	23.	C
9.	C	24.	B
10.	D	25.	D
11.	C	26.	A
12.	C	27.	B
13.	D	28.	C
14.	A	29.	C
15.	A	30.	D

TEST 2

DIRECTIONS: Each question consists of a statement. You are to indicate whether the statement is TRUE (T) or FALSE (F). *PRINT THE LETTER OF THE CORRECT ANSWER IN THE SPACE AT THE RIGHT.*

1. Baby teeth have roots.   1.____

2. The normal permanent dentition of man consists of 30 teeth.   2.____

3. It is not advisable to fill carious deciduous teeth.   3.____

4. The *dental engine* is commonly referred to as the *drill*.   4.____

5. The *styptic* is an agent which tends to stop bleeding.   5.____

6. Mouth washes will prevent dental decay.   6.____

7. In dentistry, the term *denture* generally refers to a decayed tooth.   7.____

8. The term *immunity* means non-susceptibility to a given disease.   8.____

9. Under local anesthesia, the patient generally loses consciousness during operation.   9.____

10. *Orthodontics* refers to procedures to bring irregularly positioned teeth into alignment.   10.____

11. *Prognosis* means the probable cause of disease.   11.____

12. The crown of a tooth is also known as the alveolus.   12.____

13. Rubber dam should be used wherever possible in root canal therapy.   13.____

14. Amalgam fillings are generally used for cavities in the front of the mouth.   14.____

15. A cavity may be sterilized by swabbing it with phenol.   15.____

16. Each of the 12 front teeth generally has two canals.   16.____

17. Any cavity involving only the occlusal surface of a bicuspid or molar is called a simple cavity.   17.____

18. It is good procedure to keep scissors and forceps closed when in a sterilizer.   18.____

19. Tap water is generally used for rinsing and washing x-ray films dipped in developing or fixing solutions.   19.____

20. Extra-oral rather than intra-oral dental films are used in most dental practices.   20.____

————

KEY (CORRECT ANSWERS)

1.	T		11.	F
2.	F		12.	F
3.	F		13.	T
4.	T		14.	F
5.	T		15.	T
6.	F		16.	F
7.	F		17.	T
8.	T		18.	F
9.	F		19.	T
10.	T		20.	F

EXAMINATION SECTION
TEST 1

DIRECTIONS: Each question or incomplete statement is followed by several suggested answers or completions. Select the one that BEST answers the question or completes the statement. *PRINT THE LETTER OF THE CORRECT ANSWER IN THE SPACE AT THE RIGHT.*

1. In a publicly operated dental clinic, a patient's dental record and case history should be

    A. open to the general public
    B. regarded as confidential material
    C. destroyed as soon as treatment is completed
    D. given to the patient as soon as treatment is completed

1.____

2. An appointment at a dental clinic

    A. should not be changed for any reason
    B. may be changed if the change is convenient for the patient and the dentist
    C. should not be changed without written permission of the dentist
    D. may be changed only if the patient promises faithfully to keep the new appointment

2.____

3. When answering the telephone in a dental clinic, the dental assistant should

    A. say, *Hello, who's calling, please?*
    B. inquire as to whether it is a business or personal call
    C. give the name of the clinic and identify herself
    D. let it ring at least three times before picking up the receiver

3.____

4. The MOST important reason for keeping an alphabetical file of the dental record cards of patients is so that

    A. there is a place to put every dental record card
    B. a case number can be assigned to each patient in regular order
    C. the number of patients registered at any time can be counted
    D. each patient's dental record card can be found easily

4.____

5. Of the following, the information which should be noted on a patient's dental record card after each visit to a dental clinic is the

    A. date of the visit
    B. name of the patient
    C. date of the next appointment
    D. patient's total number of visits to the clinic

5.____

6. When scheduling appointments for a dental clinic, the dental assistant must FIRST consider the

    A. day the patient wants to come to the clinic
    B. weather on the day of the appointment
    C. days on which the clinic will be open
    D. type of treatment the patient requires

6.____

7. Assume that today is Tuesday, the seventh of July.   7.____
    A patient who is given a clinic appointment for 10:30 A.M. on the seventeenth of July
    would have to come to the clinic on a

    A. Tuesday   B. Thursday   C. Friday   D. Monday

8. Assume that two patients are having an argument over which of them should be treated   8.____
    next by the dentist.
    The dental patient should

    A. ask them to let her know when they have settled the argument
    B. join the argument on the side of the weaker one
    C. tell them that because they are arguing neither one of them will be treated that day
    D. explain to them the clinic's rules about appointments and then tell them which one
       will be treated next

9. If a patient is aged, infirmed, or disabled, the dental assistant should   9.____

    A. schedule appointments at times which are convenient for the patient
    B. make appointments for him on the same days as other aged, infirmed, or disabled
       patients have their appointments
    C. allow the patient to come in at his convenience without prior appointment
    D. have the patient treated as soon as he arrives at the clinic even if another patient's
       treatment has to be interrupted

10. Suppose that a patient calls on the telephone to say that he won't be able to keep an   10.____
    appointment, which he had made previously, for a week from today.
    The BEST of the following actions for the dental assistant to take is to

    A. ask the patient why he can't keep the appointment
    B. reprimand the patient for not keeping his appointment and refuse to give him
       another
    C. tell the patient he should not have made an appointment which he wasn't going to
       keep and then make a new appointment for him
    D. thank the patient for calling and make a new appointment for him

11. Assume that because of an emergency in the dental clinic, treatment of the last patient   11.____
    will be delayed for an hour or longer.
    Under these circumstances, the BEST of the following actions for the dental hygienist
    to take is to

    A. tell the patient that schedules never work out
    B. not say anything to the patient about the delay because he might get angry
    C. ask the dentist to explain the delay to the patient
    D. tell the patient about the delay and make another appointment if he can't wait

12. Assume that a review of the attendance at a certain dental clinic showed that at many of   12.____
    the sessions there were more patients than could possibly have been treated by the den-
    tist, while at many other sessions there were fewer patients than the dentist conveniently
    could have treated.
    The MOST likely explanation for this situation is

    A. cold, rainy weather   B. poor scheduling of appointments
    C. many emergency cases   D. complications developing during treatment

13. Assume that a patient who is registered at the clinic comes in with a severe toothache but without an appointment.
The dental assistant should

    A. give him an appointment for the next day
    B. advise him to take some aspirins to relieve the pain and to come back on his regular appointment date
    C. arrange for the dentist to treat the patient as soon as possible on that day
    D. send the patient to another clinic which is not so busy

13.____

14. Assume that a patient appears at the dental clinic on the wrong day because he misunderstood the date of his appointment.
The patient should be

    A. treated by the dentist if there is time available
    B. given a small calendar and taught how to use it
    C. sent to another dental clinic for treatment that day
    D. asked to wait and then told at closing time to come back on the correct day

14.____

15. Assume that a patient undergoing a course of treatment is making a regularly scheduled visit to the dental clinic.
In order to help the dentist recall the progress of the treatment and the dental condition of the patient, the dental assistant should

    A. examine the patient's teeth before the dentist sees the patient
    B. give the dentist a list of the patient's previous appointments
    C. ask the patient to tell the dentist what has been done so far
    D. give the dentist the patient's dental record card

15.____

16. If there is a telephone call for the dentist while he is treating a patient, the dental assistant should

    A. tell the caller that the dentist is out
    B. call the dentist to the phone immediately
    C. tell the caller that the dentist is busy and offer to take a message
    D. ask the caller to hold the phone until the dentist has finished treating the patient

16.____

17. Assume that two small children are disturbing other patients in the waiting room by running around and shouting.
The dental assistant should

    A. order them out of the clinic
    B. try to interest them in a quieter activity
    C. try to quiet them by threatening to spank them
    D. ask the dentist to tell to behave themselves

17.____

18. Assume that two patients in the waiting room get involved in a loud argument about current events.
The dental assistant should

    A. tell them they are both wrong as to the matter under discussion
    B. shout at them, *Keep quiet!*
    C. ignore the argument and continue to work
    D. ask them to speak a little more quietly

18.____

19. If a patient asks the dental hygienist for advice as to whether he should follow the treat-   19.___
ment recommended by the dentist, the PROPER thing for the dental hygienist to do is to

    A. listen carefully in order to learn something about dentistry
    B. tell the patient about the details of her own dental treatment
    C. tell the patient that dental treatment should be discussed with the dentist
    D. look at the patient's dental record card to see what treatment has been received to
        date

20. If a clinic patient fails to adopt good oral hygiene practices after they have been shown to   20.___
him,

    A. this matter should be of no concern to the clinic staff
    B. continued efforts should be made to persuade the patient to adopt good practices
    C. the patient should not receive any further treatment
    D. the patient should be transferred to another clinic

21. Suppose that a patient complains to the dental hygienist about the way he has been   21.___
treated at the clinic.
The BEST of the following actions for the dental hygienist to take is to

    A. tell the patient he shouldn't complain
    B. terminate the patient's case and make no more appointments for him
    C. make a note of the complaint and tell the patient it will be looked into
    D. sympathize with the patient and tell him other patients have made the same com-
        plaint

22. Assume that a patient who has just had a tooth filled is now in the waiting room preparing   22.___
to leave. The patient states that the rough edge of the filling is causing him discomfort
and asks the dental hygienist what to do about it.
The dental hygienist should

    A. examine the filling and do whatever is necessary to make it smooth
    B. examine the filling and tell the patient what to do to make it smooth
    C. tell the patient to come back in an hour if he doesn't feel better
    D. inform the dentist of the patient's complaint

23. Of the following, the BEST time for the dental hygienist to order additional dental materi-   23.___
als and supplies is whenever

    A. the stock of some of the supplies is running low
    B. the stock of some of the supplies is exhausted
    C. there is nothing else of importance to be done in the clinic
    D. the dentist finds out what he will need for a new patient

24. The keeping of systematic records in a dental clinic is important CHIEFLY because such   24.___
records

    A. contribute substantially to the efficient operation of the clinic
    B. provide the dental hygienist with something important to do
    C. make information available for setting wage and salary rates
    D. provide information as to the number of people in need of dental treatment

25. The one of the following which is LEAST likely to be included in a monthly summary report of dental clinic activities is the

    A. name of the clinic
    B. names of the patients who were treated
    C. dates covered by the report
    D. dental work that was done in the clinic

25.____

26. If certain items which are normally included in a monthly report of dental clinic activities do not reflect credit on the dental clinic in a particular month, the dental hygienist should

    A. leave them out of that month's report
    B. change them so that they don't appear to be so bad
    C. report them as they are
    D. not submit a report for that month

26.____

27. If the dentist asks the dental hygienist to do something which she doesn't know how to do, she should

    A. refuse to do it and tell the dentist that she has more important work to do
    B. try to do it anyway, as best she can
    C. tell the dentist she would prefer to do something which she has done before
    D. tell the dentist she doesn't know how to do it and ask him how it should be done

27.____

28. If the dental assistant knows what treatment the dentist has planned for the next patient, she should

    A. tell the patient about it
    B. discourage any change in the plan
    C. prepare the proper set-up
    D. help the dentist make further plans

28.____

29. While a patient is receiving treatment in the chair, the dental hygienist should

    A. wear rubber gloves to avoid being contaminated
    B. leave the dentist and the patient alone in the operating room
    C. hand the dentist the instruments he calls for
    D. not touch the instruments until after they have been used

29.____

Questions 30-32.

DIRECTIONS: Questions 30 through 32 are to be answered on the basis of the following rules.

RULES GOVERNING CLINIC APPOINTMENTS

1. No more than eight appointments should be scheduled for each three hour clinic session for each dentist who will be on duty.

2. A new patient's first appointment should allow time for a complete examination by the dentist.

3. Appointments should not be made less than four days apart for any patient without the consent of the dentist.

4. Appointments should be made in person or over the telephone whenever possible in order that the patient may give his consent while the appointment is being made. If a request for an appointment is made in any other manner, it must contain a statement of the date(s) and time(s) acceptable to the patient in order to be approved. No patient shall be given an appointment to which he does not consent.

5. A card stating the place, date, and time of the appointment shall be given to or mailed to the patient on the same day on which the appointment is made.

6. If a patient fails to keep three appointments in a row, his case is to be terminated and no further appointments are to be made for him unless a new authorization is received.

30. A patient who requests an appointment at a clinic session for which eight patients are already scheduled for each dentist who will be on duty should be   30._____

    A. given the appointment since he has already consented to it
    B. told that he cannot be given an appointment at that clinic session
    C. given an appointment at another session without his consent
    D. told to come in without an appointment and hope for a cancellation

31. It would be IMPROPER for a patient to be given appointments on three successive days   31._____
if the

    A. schedule for each of those days is already partly filled
    B. dentist has treated the patient only once previously
    C. patient has requested the appointments by mail
    D. dentist does not give his consent to the appointments

32. A patient who has failed to keep three successive appointments should   32._____

    A. be sent a card stating the place, date, and time of the next appointment
    B. not be given another appointment without a new authorization
    C. be given an emergency appointment for a clinic session which already has eight patients scheduled
    D. not be given another appointment unless he appears in person to make it

33. The word *identify* means MOST NEARLY   33._____

    A. excuse   B. label   C. leave   D. inoculate

34. The word *masticate* means MOST NEARLY   34._____

    A. chew   B. overcome   C. inflame   D. enlarge

35. The word *sedative* means MOST NEARLY   35._____

    A. poisonous   B. sterile
    C. stimulating   D. quieting

36. The standard number of permanent teeth in normal human adults is   36._____

    A. 28   B. 32   C. 35   D. 40

37. Deciduous teeth are teeth that USUALLY erupt _____ four years of life.   37._____

    A. in the first   B. in the second
    C. in the third   D. after the third

38. Of the following, the condition which is an example of malocclusion is a(n)   38._____

    A. filled molar   B. overbite
    C. gingival crevice   D. extracted bicuspid

39. The branch of dentistry that deals with the prevention and correction of irregularities of   39._____
the teeth and dental arches is known as

    A. periodontics   B. orthodontics
    C. prosthodontics   D. endodontics

40. The condition known as caries refers to   40._____

    A. decay of the teeth
    B. deterioration of the gums
    C. inflammation of the cartilage
    D. irritation of the tissues of the cheeks

41. A complete replacement of the upper or lower teeth is called a(n)   41._____

    A. artificial denture   B. single hung bridge
    C. matrix band   D. articulator

42. The sequence of exploration, excavation, preparation, and restoration has to do MAINLY   42._____
with the treatment of

    A. pyorrhea   B. gingivitis
    C. caries   D. malocclusion

43. Acids are believed to be a major factor in tooth decay. In order to limit the formation of   43._____
these acids, the BEST time to brush the teeth is immediately

    A. before eating
    B. after eating
    C. upon waking in the morning
    D. before retiring at night

44. Of the following items, the one which is NOT part of a modern dental unit is the   44._____

    A. cuspidor   B. warm air syringe
    C. impression tray   D. foot controller

45. The one of the following items which is NOT part of a standard dental chair is the 45.____

    A. raising lever
    B. tilting lever
    C. cantilever
    D. backrest adjusting lever

46. The device used by dentists to enable them to see obscure tooth areas is a(n) 46.____

    A. tooth refractor   B. explorer
    C. angulator   D. mouth mirror

47. Of the following, the one which is NOT a type of hand-piece is a _____ angle. 47.____

    A. contra-   B. right   C. straight   D. turn

48. A pestle is USUALLY used with a 48.____

    A. bur   B. matrix retainer
    C. mouth mirror   D. mortar

49. Of the following, the item which is NOT used to keep the site of a dental operation dry is 49.____
    a

    A. mouth piece   B. rubber dam
    C. cotton roll   D. saliva ejector

50. Dental hatchets, hoes, and chisels are types of 50.____

    A. cutting instruments   B. burnishing instruments
    C. explorers   D. burs

KEY (CORRECT ANSWERS)

1.	B	11.	D	21.	C	31.	D	41.	A
2.	B	12.	B	22.	D	32.	B	42.	C
3.	C	13.	C	23.	A	33.	B	43.	B
4.	D	14.	A	24.	A	34.	A	44.	C
5.	A	15.	D	25.	B	35.	D	45.	C
6.	C	16.	C	26.	C	36.	B	46.	D
7.	C	17.	B	27.	D	37.	A	47.	D
8.	D	18.	D	28.	C	38.	B	48.	D
9.	A	19.	C	29.	A	39.	B	49.	A
10.	D	20.	B	30.	B	40.	A	50.	A

TEST 2

DIRECTIONS: Each question or incomplete statement is followed by several suggested answers or completions. Select the one that BEST answers the question or completes the statement. *PRINT THE LETTER OF THE CORRECT ANSWER IN THE SPACE AT THE RIGHT.*

1. The dental instrument whose purpose is to remove the roots of teeth is the

   A. retractor
   C. excavator
   B. elevator
   D. spader

   1.____

2. A burnisher is USUALLY used on an amalgam filling to _____ it.

   A. burn
   B. remove
   C. smooth
   D. harden

   2.____

3. The one of the following which is NOT used in modern dentistry in connection with the handpiece is the

   A. rasp
   B. bur
   C. stone
   D. disk

   3.____

4. Of the following instruments, the one which, when used, must come into direct contact with the tooth that is being treated is the

   A. retractor
   C. extracting forceps
   B. cotton pliers
   D. spatula

   4.____

5. The CHIEF difference between a sealer and an excavator is that a(n)

   A. excavator has a cutting edge while a scaler does not
   B. scaler has a cutting edge while an excavator does not
   C. scaler has an entirely smooth surface while an excavator has a roughened surface
   D. scaler is electrically powered while an excavator is not

   5.____

6. The instrument which would usually be MOST useful for excavating a cavity is a(n)

   A. burnisher
   C. explorer
   B. bur
   D. elevator

   6.____

7. The one of the following which is NOT a commonly used dental cement is _____ cement.

   A. zinc and phosphate
   C. silicate
   B. rubber
   D. zinc oxide-eugenol

   7.____

8. The one of the following which is MOST essential in making a model of the lower teeth in a patient's mouth is a(n)

   A. mortar
   C. plugger
   B. Dappen dish
   D. impression tray

   8.____

9. A Dappen dish is used to hold

   A. medicaments
   C. plaster of Paris
   B. paper disks
   D. hot ashes

   9.____

10. Plaster of Paris is NEVER used in making

    A. impressions
    C. implaners
    B. inlays
    D. investments

    10.____

11. The PROPER method of mixing plaster of Paris is to   11.____

    A. pour the water into the bowl first and then add the powder
    B. place the powder in the bowl first and then add the water
    C. put the water and the powder into the bowl at the same time
    D. place a little powder in the bowl and then add some water; then add more powder and then more water in small quantities until the necessary amount is mixed

12. Of the following, the MOST generally satisfactory substance for use as a denture base material is   12.____

    A. platinum   B. acetate   C. gold foil   D. acrylic

13. Procaine hydrochloride, Metycaine with epinephrine, Intracaine with epinephrine, and Xylocaine hydrochloride are all   13.____

    A. chemical sterilizing tablets
    B. medicated pills
    C. oral prophylactic solutions
    D. local anesthetic solutions

14. On a modern dental x-ray machine, the duration of each exposure is controlled directly by a   14.____

    A. foot pedal   B. stop watch
    C. preset timer   D. slide rule

15. When dental x-rays are taken, the film should be held in place during the exposure period by the (a)   15.____

    A. dentist   B. metal clamp
    C. dental hygienist   D. rinn/or other x-ray holder

16. The one of the following phases of processing exposed x-ray film in which sodium thio-sulfate, commonly known as hypo, is used is   16.____

    A. developing   B. fixing
    C. washing   D. drying

17. The one of the following procedures which is ACCEPTABLE in the preparation of an amalgam is to   17.____

    A. start with a mercury to amalgam alloy ratio which is higher than the manufacturer's specifications
    B. start with a mercury to amalgam alloy ratio which is lower than the manufacturer's specifications
    C. add more mercury to the amalgam at a later state of the manipulations
    D. mix or mull the amalgam in the palm of the hand

18. It is generally considered to be good practice to mix dental cement   18.____

    A. at least fifteen minutes before using it
    B. in a mortar
    C. on a chilled slab
    D. in a Dappen dish

19. When using a boiling-type sterilizer, it is PREFERABLE to use distilled water instead of tap water in order to   19._____

    A. increase the temperature
    B. reduce corrosion
    C. keep a constant water level
    D. completely submerge the instruments

20. The active sterilizing agent in an autoclave is   20._____

    A. formaldehyde   B. saturated steam
    C. hot oil   D. boiling water

21. When a number of dental instruments have been sterilized together, the BEST of the following actions for the dental hygienist to take is to   21._____

    A. put them all away in the same place
    B. leave them in the sterilizer to keep them sterile
    C. sort them and put them away in the appropriate places
    D. hand them to the dentist as soon as they are cool

22. Dental instruments and materials should be inventoried   22._____

    A. at regular intervals
    B. when there are a number of patients in the clinic
    C. when the supply runs low
    D. immediately after a supply requisition has been completed

Questions 23-28.

DIRECTIONS: Questions 23 through 28 are to be answered on the basis of the usual rules of filing. Column I lists, next to the numbers 23 to 28, the names of 6 children whose treatment has been completed in the Dental Clinic at the Municipal Health Center. Column II lists, next to the letters A to L, the headings of the drawers of the inactive file into which you are to place the records of these children. In the space at the right, next to the number preceding each name listed in Column I, print the letter preceding the heading of the file drawer in which the record should be filed. The following sample is given to show how these questions should be answered:
Sample: George Clark
The record of George Clark should be filed in the drawer marked *Cip-Cof*. The answer, therefore, is F.

COLUMN I   COLUMN II

23. Raye Corrigan   A. Caa - Cal   23._____
24. John Chang   B. Cam - Cem   24._____
25. Charles Czynchic   C. Cen - Chi   25._____
26. Alice Cahn   D. Chj - Cib   26._____
27. Thomas Cuneo   E. Cic - Cio   27._____
28. Gwen Civet   F. Cip - Cof   28._____
                                    G. Cog - Cor
                                    H. Cos - Cul
                                    I. Cum - Cus
                                    J. Cut - Cyc
                                    K. Cyd - Cyz
                                    L. Cza - Czy

Questions 29-34.

DIRECTIONS: In answering Questions 29 through 34, alphabetize the four names listed in each question; then print in the space at the right the item number for the correct sequence of the four letters preceding the alphabetized names to show the correct alphabetical arrangement of the four names. The following sample is presented to show how the questions should be answered:

Sample: A. John Smith (4)
B. Jane Jones (2)
C. John Doe (1)
D. Jane Roberts (3)

The CORRECT sequence is:
A. ABCD   B. BDCA   C. CADB   D. CBDA

The numbers in parentheses indicate the proper alphabetical order in which these names should be filed. The answer, therefore, is CBDA, or item D.

29. A. Mrs. Marsha Lindsey   B. Miss Alice Tolachi   29.___
C. Mrs. Clara Reiner   D. Mr. Roger Nelson
The CORRECT sequence is:
A. ABCD   B. ADCB   C. CDAB   D. DABC

30. A. John Aronson   B. James Aronson   30.___
C. George Aarons   D. Adam Amberson
The CORRECT sequence is:
A. BCAD   B. CABC   C. DBAC   D. CDBA

31. A. Nathan Persky   B. Alfred Parsons   31.___
C. Bernard Parks   D. Arthur Parkinson
The CORRECT sequence is:
A. BACD   B. CBDA   C. DCBA   D. ACDB

32. A. Sara Schwartz   B. Sarah Salvia   32.___
C. Jean Sampson   D. Janet Shultze
The CORRECT sequence is:
A. BDCA   B. BCAD   C. CDAB   D. BADC

33. A. J.D. Cavanagh   B. Charles A. Coca   33.___
C. Harold E. Coe   D. Fred T. Cavan
The CORRECT sequence is:
A. DABC   B. ADBC   C. DCBA   D. ACDB

34. A. Charles A. Wolff   B. Chas. A. Wolfe   34.___
C. Charles F. Wolf   D. C.H. Wolfson
The CORRECT sequence is:
A. BDAC   B. ACDB   C. DBAC   D. CBAD

Questions 35-41.

DIRECTIONS: Questions 35 through 41 are to be answered on the basis of the information in the following table.

DENTAL SUPPLY INVENTORY TALLY SHEET AND REQUISITION GUIDE
AS OF NOVEMBER 30

Item	Catalog Number	Quantity in Stock	Unit of Measure	Minimum Stock Level	Full Stock Level
Amalgam alloy	aa-01	2	ounce	3	6
Burs	bu-22	18	each	24	36
Cement liquid	cl-07	1	bottle	2	4
Cotton rolls	cr-12	8	box	6	12
Explorers	ex-16	20	each	10	20
Impression material	im-05	15	tin	8	20
Mercury	me-01	2	bottle	2	4
Novocaine	an-06	14	ampule	12	24
Plaster of Paris	pl-04	1	box	2	8
Scalers	sc-11	18	each	10	20
Spatulas	sp-03	3	each	6	12
X-ray film	xf-24	7	dozen	6	9

35. The item whose catalog number is ex-16 is listed in the Dental Supply Inventory Tally Sheet as

    A. x-ray film   B. explorers
    C. cotton rolls   D. amalgam alloy

35._____

36. On the basis of the Dental Supply Inventory Tally Sheet shown above, the combined total of scalers, burs, and explorers in stock as of November 30 is

    A. 24   B. 48   C. 56   D. 72

36._____

37. As of November 30, the total quantity of the items in stock which come in tins, ampules, and boxes is

    A. 9   B. 16   C. 27   D. 38

37._____

38. If the full stock level of all items whose unit of measure is *box* were increased by 25%, the total quantity of such items at the full stock level would be MOST NEARLY

    A. 20   B. 25   C. 30   D. 40

38._____

39. As of November 30, the total quantity of items which would have to be requisitioned in order to bring up to full stock level all items whose unit of measure is *each* is MOST NEARLY

    A. 29   B. 36   C. 40   D. 46

39._____

40. Assume that you have been instructed to requisition enough of each item which is below   40.____
the minimum stock level listed in the table to bring the clinic's supplies up to the full stock
level of that item.
The one of the following choices which contains an item that should be ordered and
the correct amount of the order is

    A.   impression material - 7   B.   spatulas - 9
    C.   novocaine - 10   D.   burs - 6

41. Assume that you have been instructed to order supplies whenever the quantity in stock   41.____
falls below the minimum stock level listed in the table for each item.
The one of the following groups which lists only those items which should be ordered
as of November 30 is

    A.   cement liquid, impression material, plaster of Paris
    B.   spatulas, plaster of Paris, amalgam alloy
    C.   mercury, cement liquid, cotton rolls
    D.   burs, explorers, novocaine

Question 42.

DIRECTIONS: Question 42 is to be answered on the basis of the following paragraph.

The same amount of skill must be employed in restoring primary and young permanent
teeth as is used in the adult dentition. Speed is of great importance when operating on children. It is here that the dental hygienist can play a very important role. The hygienist who is
thoroughly trained in working with children will materially reduce the operating time of the
dentist. The dental hygienist is no doubt a greater help with the child patient than with the
adult.

42. On the basis of the above statement, we may conclude MOST NEARLY that   42.____

    A.   a dental hygienist is of no help to the dentist who is working with an adult patient
    B.   when working on children, it is not important to work as quickly as when working on
        adults
    C.   when assisted by a well-trained dental hygienist, the dentist's working time on chil-
        dren can be made shorter
    D.   dentists cannot work without dental hygienists

Questions 43-46.

DIRECTIONS: Questions 43 through 46 are to be answered on the basis of the following
               paragraph.

The ideal storage space for most supplies is in a cabinet or closet. A cabinet in the laboratory and some of the drawers in the dental cabinet in the operating room may be utilized for storing part of the supplies, such as cement liquids. Certain supplies should not be stored in the supply cabinet. For example, x-ray films should be placed in a lead-lined box designed for that purpose. Films may be exposed prematurely if they are near the x-ray machine and unprotected. Antibiotics should be kept in cold storage to maintain their efficacy. Instructions on the package will give this information. Acids, such as hydrochloric and sulfuric, are stored separately. Fumes from acids may cause corrosion or damage to metals and other supplies. Gold and other precious metals should be kept in a strong box or safe. As plaster and stone are bulky, such materials can be kept in the janitor's closet or in a back room which is dry and away from moisture. Inflammable items, such as ether or ethyl chloride, must be kept away from heat and flame. The assistant should acquaint herself with those supplies which have a limited shelf life and should plan to use those items first which have been on the shelf the longest.

43. On the basis of the above paragraph, the MOST accurate of the following statements   43.____
with respect to the handling of x-ray films is that they should be

    A. unpacked and stored near the x-ray machine
    B. unpacked upon arrival and counted for accuracy
    C. kept in a well-heated supply closet
    D. stored in a specially designed lead-lined box

44. On the basis of the above paragraph, the one of the following items which may MOST   44.____
properly be stored in the dental cabinet in the operating room is

    A. hydrochloric acid   B. platinum or gold foil
    C. plaster of Paris   D. cement liquids

45. On the basis of the above paragraph, the MOST accurate of the following statements   45.____
with respect to the storing of antibiotics is that

    A. the dental hygienist should use her own judgment as to how these supplies should
       be stored
    B. they should be kept under refrigeration in accordance with the special instructions
       on the package
    C. such items should be kept in a warm cabinet to maintain their efficacy
    D. they may be stored in a cabinet in the laboratory along with other supplies with a
       limited shelf life

46. On the basis of the above paragraph, the MOST accurate of the following statements   46.____
with respect to ethyl chloride is that

    A. it should be kept in a back room which is dry
    B. it is an inflammable item
    C. the fumes from ethyl chloride may cause corrosion to metals
    D. it has a limited shelf life

Questions 47-50.

DIRECTIONS: Questions 47 through 50 are to be answered on the basis of the accompanying diagram. For each question, print in the space alongside each of the numbers 47 through 50 the capital letter which, on the diagram, represents the part or structure named in that question.

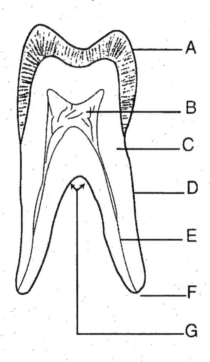

47. Dentin   47.____

48. Enamel   48.____

49. Pulp canal   49.____

50. Pulp chamber   50.____

———

KEY (CORRECT ANSWERS)

1.	B	11.	A	21.	C	31.	C	41.	B
2.	C	12.	D	22.	A	32.	B	42.	C
3.	A	13.	D	23.	G	33.	A	43.	D
4.	C	14.	C	24.	C	34.	D	44.	D
5.	B	15.	D	25.	L	35.	B	45.	B
6.	B	16.	B	26.	A	36.	C	46.	B
7.	B	17.	A	27.	I	37.	D	47.	C
8.	D	18.	C	28.	F	38.	B	48.	A
9.	A	19.	B	29.	B	39.	A	49.	E
10.	C	20.	B	30.	D	40.	B	50.	B

———

EXAMINATION SECTION

TEST 1

DIRECTIONS: Each question or incomplete statement is followed by several suggested answers or completions. Select the one that BEST answers the question or completes the statement. *PRINT THE LETTER OF THE CORRECT ANSWER IN THE SPACE AT THE RIGHT.*

1.   Which of the following medications would be contraindicated for a patient with severe hypertension?
    A. Fluoride   B. Nitrous oxide
    C. Epinephrine   D. Lidocaine

1.____

2.   What type of anesthetic should be used if a patient is going to undergo a procedure that will last approximately 30 minutes?
    A. Mepivacaine with epinephrine   B. Bupivacaine with epinephrine
    C. Prilocaine with epinephrine   D. Lidocaine HCl

2.____

3.   Which instrument comes in various types including straight, binangle, Wedelstaedt, and angle-former?
    A, Chisel   B. Hatchet   C. Excavator   D. Hoe

3.____

4.   If you notice demineralization of the enamel on the lingual of anterior teeth, what is the underlying cause?
    A. Diabetes   B. Hyperthyroidism
    C. Anorexia   D. Bulimia

4.____

5.   Which of the following is the surface of the tooth toward the midline?
    A. Mesial   B. Distal   C. Lingual   D. Buccal

5.____

6.   Which of the following is the portion of the tooth that is covered with enamel?
    A. Anatomical   B. Proximal   C. Apical   D. Cervical

6.____

7.   What is the depth of a normal sulcus?
    A. 1-2 mm   B. 2-3 mm   C. 3-4 mm   D. 4-5 mm

7.____

8.   What impression material is used to take impressions for study models?
    A. Plaster   B. Alginate   C. Arginate   D. Calcitrate

8.____

9.   What material is used to pour the impression for study models?
    A. Plaster   B. Alginate
    C. Elastomers   D. Zinc oxide eugenol

9.____

10.   Which artery is used to monitor blood pressure in the dental office?
    A. Carotid   B. Brachial   C. Cephalic   D. Mesenteric

10.____

11. In an emergency situation, what artery is used to monitor pulse rate?   11.____
    A. Carotid   B. Brachial   C. Cephalic   D. Mesenteric

12. If the patient is reclined at 45 degrees, on what quadrant would the dentist   12.____
    be working?
    A. 1 and 2   B. 2 and 3   C. 3 and 4   D. 1 and 4

13. At what clock position is the dental assistant seated for a right-handed   13.____
    dentist?
    A. 12 – 2 o'clock   B. 2 – 4 o'clock   C. 6 – 8 o'clock   D. 8 – 10 o'clock

14. At what clock position is the dental assistant seated for a left-handed   14.____
    dentist?
    A. 12 – 2 o'clock   B. 2 – 4 o'clock   C. 6 – 8 o'clock   D. 8 – 10 o'clock

15. What fingers are used to place instruments into the dentist's hand?   15.____
    A. Second finger, ring finger, and pinky
    B. Index finger, second finger, and ring finger
    C. Thumb, index finger, and pinky
    D. Thumb, index finger, and second finger

16. What fingers are used to retrieve dental instruments from the dentist?   16.____
    A. Thumb and index finger   B. Thumb and second finger
    C. Second finger and ring finger   D. Ring finger and pinky

17. In which zone should the instrument tray be located?   17.____
    A. Static   B. Assistant   C. Transfer   D. Operator

18. The area below the patient's nose where instruments are passed and   18.____
    received is referred to as the _____ zone.
    A. static   B. assistant   C. transfer   D. operator

19. Which of the following is the CORRECT placement for the HVE tip?   19.____
    A. Superior to the tooth being worked on
    B. Inferior to the tooth being worked on
    C. One tooth distal to the tooth being worked on
    D. One tooth proximal to the tooth being worked on

20. Where should cotton rolls be placed when treating mandibular teeth?   20.____
    A. Mesially   B. Distally   C. Lingually   D. Buccally

21. Where should cotton rolls be placed when treating maxillary teeth?   21.____
    A. Mesially   B. Distally   C. Lingually   D. Buccally

22. A permanent dentition consists of how many teeth?   22.____
    A. 30   B. 32   C. 34   D. 36

23. Which teeth, shown in the image at the right, are commonly referred to as the "eye teeth"?
    A. Premolars
    B. Canines
    C. Incisors
    D. Bicuspids

23.____

24. A permanent dentition consists of how many premolars?
    A. 2   B. 4   C. 8   D. 12

24.____

25. Using the Universal System of tooth designation, what is tooth #22?
    A. Upper left central incisor   B. Upper right lateral incisor
    C. Lower left canine   D. Lower right canine

25.____

26. Using the International Standards Organization system of tooth recording, what is tooth #25?
    A. Lower left central incisor   B. Lower right central incisor
    C. Upper left second premolar   D. Upper right second premolar

26.____

27. Using Black's classification of cavities, a pit lesion on the buccal of molars and premolars is considered a class _____ restoration or cavity.
    A. I   B. II   C. III   D. IV

27.____

28. Which of the following refers to any tooth that remains unerupted in the jaw beyond the time at which it should normally erupt?
    A. Fused   B. Abraded   C. Impacted   D. Cemented

28.____

29. The high-speed contra-angle handpiece reaches a speed of _____ rpm.
    A. 150,000   B. 250,000   C. 350,000   D. 450,000

29.____

30. In the United States, nitrous oxide gas lines are what color?
    A. Red   B. Blue   C. Green   D. Black

30.____

KEY (CORRECT ANSWERS)

1.	C	11.	A	21.	D
2.	D	12.	C	22.	B
3.	A	13.	B	23.	B
4.	D	14.	D	24.	C
5.	A	15.	D	25.	C
6.	A	16.	D	26.	C
7.	B	17.	A	27.	A
8.	B	18.	C	28.	C
9.	A	19.	C	29.	D
10.	B	20.	C	30.	B

TEST 2

DIRECTIONS: Each question or incomplete statement is followed by several suggested answers or completions. Select the one that BEST answers the question or completes the statement. *PRINT THE LETTER OF THE CORRECT ANSWER IN THE SPACE AT THE RIGHT.*

1. Which of the following is a condition which will result if an alginate impression absorbs additional water by being stored in water or in a very wet paper towel?
   A. Imbibition
   B. Hydrolysis
   C. Polymerization
   D. Dessication

   1.____

2. Which of the following waxes can be applied to the edge of the alginate trays to improve the fit of the tray?
   A. Utility
   B. Inlay
   C. Casting
   D. Baseplate

   2.____

3. Which of the following is defined as moving the tooth back and forth within the socket?
   A. Pronation
   B. Supination
   C. Luxation
   D. Capitation

   3.____

4. What type of forceps is designed to grasp the bifurcation of the root of a mandibular molar?
   A. Curved
   B. Bayonet
   C. Cowhorn
   D. Universal

   4.____

5. Which instrument would be used to measure the depth of the gingival sulcus?
   A. Cowhorn explorer
   B. Shepherd's hook
   C. Periodontal explorer
   D. Right angle explorer

   5.____

6. Which instrument, shown in the image at the right, has a sharp round angular tip used to detect tooth anomalies?
   A. Cowhorn explorer
   B. Shepherd's hook
   C. Periodontal explorer
   D. Right angle explorer

   6.____

7. Which instrument is commonly used to scale surfaces in the anterior region of the mouth?
   A. Curet scaler
   B. Gracey scaler
   C. Straight sickle scaler
   D. Modified sickle scaler

   7.____

8. Which instrument, shown in the image at the right, is used to scale deep periodontal pockets or furcation areas?
   A. Curet scaler
   B. Gracey scaler
   C. Straight sickle scaler
   D. Modified sickle scaler

8.____

9. Where should the HVE tip be positioned when the operator is working on the labial of tooth #9?
   A. In the vestibule
   B. I the retromolar area
   C. On the opposite side of the tooth being prepared
   D. On the labial surface of the tooth being prepared

9.____

10. If a right-handed dentist is doing preparation on #30 MO, the dental assistant should place the HVE tip on the
    A. buccal of #30   B. buccal of #19
    C. lingual of #30   D. lingual of #19

10.____

11. The cement that has a sedative effect on the pulp is known as
    A. glass ionomer   B. zinc phosphate
    C. zinc oxide eugenol   D. zinc silicon phosphate

11.____

12. Which of the following techniques would be useful for caries removal?
    A. No. ¼ FG and explorer
    B. No. ¼ FG and spoon excavator
    C. No. 2 RA bur and spoon excavator
    D. No. 2 RA bur and enamel hatchet

12.____

13. Which part of the anesthetic syringe is different among the aspirating and non-aspirating varieties?
    A. Piston   B. Harpoon
    C. Syringe barrel   D. Metal thumb ring

13.____

14. For what purpose would a tooth be acid etched when using a composite restorative?
    A. To prepare the pulp
    B. To seal the dentinal tubules
    C. To form tags on the etched tooth surface
    D. To form a bond on the cavity structure of the tooth

14.____

15. Which of the following is an indication for pit and fissure sealants?
    A. Teeth are prone to caries.
    B. Teeth are not prone to caries.
    C. Teeth have sealants already present.
    D. The fossae are wide and easy to clean.

15.____

16. If a tooth has been avulsed, the tooth has been   16.____
    A. fractured   B. sealed with a sealant
    C. restored with amalgam   D. knocked free from the oral cavity

17. Which of the following is the MOST common type of attachment for fixed   17.____
    orthodontic appliances?
    A. Separator   B. Arch wire
    C. Bonded bracket   D. Orthodontic band

18. Which of the following is a thermoplastic material used to stabilize an   18.____
    anterior clamp?
    A. Floss   B. Dri-angle
    C. Sticky wax   D. Dental compound

19. What type of cement must be mixed on a glass slab?   19.____
    A. Calcium hydroxide   B. Zinc phosphate
    C. Zinc oxide eugenol   D. Zinc polycarbonate

20. What material is recommended for polishing filled hybrid composites and   20.____
    resin restorations?
    A. Tin oxide paste   B. Aluminum oxide paste
    C. Diamond polishing paste   D. Coarse polishing paste

21. Composite restorative materials are usually cured for what period of time   21.____
    with a halogen curing light?
    A. 3 seconds   B. 20 seconds   C. 60 seconds   D. 120 seconds

22. What instrument is used when ligating an archwire?   22.____
    A. Hemostats   B. Howe pliers
    C. Utility pliers   D. Ligature tying pliers

23. A periodontal probe is an example of what type of instrument?   23.____
    A. Accessory   B. Restorative   C. Examination   D. Hand cutting

24. Which of the following statements is TRUE regarding the angle of the   24.____
    bevel of the HVE tip?
    It should be
    A. parallel to the occlusal surface
    B. perpendicular to the occlusal surface
    C. parallel to the buccal and lingual surfaces
    D. perpendicular to the buccal and lingual surfaces

25. The tip of the composite curing light should be held at an angle of _____ 25.____
    degrees to the tooth.
    A. 10   B. 30   C. 45   D. 60

26. Which of the following is defined as a negative impression of the patient's 26.____
    dental arch?
    A. Die   B. Model   C. Cast   D. Impression

27. Which of the following refers to the process by which the resin material
is changed from a pliable state to a hardened restoration?
    A. Microcuring   B. Macrocuring
    C. Light curing   D. Endothermic curing

27._____

28. Which of the following are the only nutrients that can build and repair
body tissues?
    A. Proteins   B. Vitamins   C. Minerals   D. Carbohydrates

28._____

29. If a patient is prescribed to take a medication once every other day, what
is the APPROPRIATE abbreviation for this prescription?
    A. q.d.   B. q.i.d.   C. q.o.d.   D. t.i.d.

29._____

30. Inflammation of the supporting tissues of the teeth that begins with gingivitis
can progress into the connective tissue and alveolar bone that supports the
teeth and become which of the following?
    A. Glossitis   B. Gangrene   C. Periodontitis   D. Epiglottitis

30._____

KEY (CORRECT ANSWERS)

1.	A	11.	C	21.	B
2.	A	12.	C	22.	D
3.	C	13.	B	23.	A
4.	C	14.	C	24.	C
5.	C	15.	A	25.	A
6.	A	16.	D	26.	D
7.	C	17.	C	27.	C
8.	B	18.	D	28.	A
9.	C	19.	B	29.	C
10.	C	20.	B	30.	C

TEST 3

DIRECTIONS: Each question or incomplete statement is followed by several suggested answers or completions. Select the one that BEST answers the question or completes the statement. *PRINT THE LETTER OF THE CORRECT ANSWER IN THE SPACE AT THE RIGHT.*

1.   Subgingival calculus occurs below the gingival margin and can be _____ in color because of subgingival bleeding?
    A. Red   B. Grey   C. Black   D. Yellow

    1.____

2.   In which of the following procedures could the patient be placed in an upright position?
    A. Composite procedure
    B. Removal of a posterior tooth
    C. Taking a diagnostic impression
    D. Polishing the teeth after a prophylaxis

    2.____

3.   Which of the following would be the MOST common indication for placing pit and fissure sealants?
    A. Posterior teeth with deep pits and fissures
    B. All erupted permanent molars and premolars
    C. Posterior teeth with small areas of early caries
    D. As a preventative measure for partially erupted teeth

    3.____

4.   What microorganism must be present for caries formation to begin?
    A. Streptococcus pneumoniae   B. Klebsiella pneumoniae
    C. Candida albicans   D. Streptococcus mutans

    4.____

5.   Which of the following is the MOST common form of fluoride used with the rigid tray system?
    A. Sodium fluoride   B. Stannous fluoride paste
    C. Liquid fluoride supplements   D. Acidulated phosphate fluoride gel

    5.____

6.   Which of the following statements are TRUE regarding a vulcanite bur?
    A. It smooths roughness in metals.
    B. It grossly reduces an acrylic prosthesis.
    C. It grossly reduces a metal prosthesis.
    D. It polishes acrylic prosthesis with pumice.

    6.____

7.   What type of curette has two cutting edges?
    A. Sickle   B. Gracey   C. Kirkland   D. Universal

    7.____

8.   What type of file is recommended for canal enlargement?
    A. Pesso   B. Broach   C. Reamer   D. Hedstrom

    8.____

9. The main component in the liquid of zinc phosphate is
   A. zinc oxide
   B. acetic acid
   C. phosphoric acid
   D. hydrogen peroxide

   9._____

10. Which supplemental material is contraindicated under composite resins and glass ionomer restorations?
    A. Varnish
    B. Etchant
    C. Dentin sealer
    D. Calcium hydroxide

    10._____

11. Calcium hydroxide is typically placed on what structure of the tooth?
    A. Pulp
    B. Dentin
    C. Enamel
    D. Cementum

    11._____

12. Which of the following is the technical term for a Class III occlusion?
    A. Distoclusion
    B. Malocclusion
    C. Mesioclusion
    D. Functional occlusion

    12._____

13. What type of impression material should NOT be mixed while wearing latex gloves?
    A. Polyether
    B. Polysulfide
    C. Hydrocolloid
    D. Condensation silicone

    13._____

14. Which of the following is the type of fixed prosthesis that only has one abutment?
    A. Partial denture
    B. Maryland bridge
    C. Cantilever bridge
    D. Temporary bridge

    14._____

15. The rounded raised area on the cervical third of the lingual surface of anterior teeth is referred to as
    A. abrasion
    B. mamelon
    C. cingulum
    D. imbrication

    15._____

16. Which of the following is an absorbable suture material?
    A. Silk
    B. Nylon
    C. Plain catgut
    D. Polyester fiber

    16._____

17. Sealant material should NOT be stored in proximity to any products containing which of the following?
    A. Eugenol
    B. Acrylate
    C. BIS-GMA
    D. Sodium bicarbonate

    17._____

18. Which of the following is a treatment that is used as an attempt to save the pulp and encourage the formation of dentin at the site of an injury?
    A. Pulpotomy
    B. Pulpectomy
    C. Apicoectomy
    D. Pulp capping

    18._____

19. Which of the following cements has an acidic quality that may be irritating to the pulp?
    A. Glass ionomer
    B. Zinc phosphate
    C. Zinc carboxylate
    D. Zinc oxide eugenol

    19._____

20. What level of consciousness is a patient at during general anesthesia? 20.____
    A. Stage I   B. Stage II   C. Stage III   D. Stage IV

21. When setting up an instrument tray or cassette with instruments, how should 21.____
    the instruments be set up?
    A. From right to left   B. From left to right
    C. From top to bottom   D. From bottom to top

22. The assistant's stool should be positioned 4-6 inches 22.____
    A. below the dentist   B. above the dentist
    C. away from the patient   D. above the patient

23. A base is placed in which location of a cavity preparation? 23.____
    A. Cavity wall   B. Pulpal floor
    C. Proximal wall   D. Enamel margin

24. Zinc oxide eugenol should be prepared on what type of mixing pad? 24.____
    A. Glass   B. Plastic
    C. Ceramic tile   D. Treated paper pad

25. Which of the following lines refers to developmental horizontal lines on 25.____
    anterior teeth?
    A. Incisal   B. Oblique   C. Marginal   D. Imbrication

26. Under what condition can a post-extraction dressing be used? 26.____
    A. Only after 3rd molar extractions
    B. When there is loss of the blood clot
    C. Any time after a surgical incision
    D. When blood begins to ooze from the alveolus

27. Which medical condition, illustrated 27.____
    in the image at the right, is
    characterized by the mandible
    being located ahead of the maxilla?
    A. Retrusion
    B. Prognathism
    C. Micrognathism
    D. Macrognathism

28. Which of the following refers to a living jaw bone naturally growing 28.____
    around an implant?
    A. Osteomalacia   B. Osteomyelitis
    C. Osseointegration   D. Osteogenesis

29. Which restorative material releases fluoride?   29.____
    A. Glass ionomer   B. Amalgam   C. Ceramic   D. Cast-gold

30. What type of dentin forms throughout the life of the tooth, resulting in a   30.____
    narrowing of the pulp chamber?
    A. Primary   B. Secondary   C. Reparative   D. Constrictive

---

KEY (CORRECT ANSWERS)

1.	C	11.	B	21.	B
2.	C	12.	C	22.	B
3.	D	13.	D	23.	B
4.	D	14.	C	24.	A
5.	D	15.	C	25.	D
6.	B	16.	C	26.	B
7.	D	17.	A	27.	B
8.	D	18.	D	28.	C
9.	C	19.	B	29.	A
10.	A	20.	C	30.	B

TEST 4

DIRECTIONS: Each question or incomplete statement is followed by several suggested answers or completions. Select the one that BEST answers the question or completes the statement. *PRINT THE LETTER OF THE CORRECT ANSWER IN THE SPACE AT THE RIGHT.*

1. What feature do newly erupted central and lateral incisors have on the incisal edge?   1._____
    A. Abrasions   B. Mamelons   C. Cingula   D. Imbrications

2. Pain is transmitted through dentin through   2._____
    A. nerves   B. dentin fibers
    C. dentin tubules   D. odontoblasts

3. What dental instruments are more commonly referred to by a number rather than a name?   3._____
    A. Pliers   B. Mirrors
    C. Excavators   D. Restorative instruments

4. What type of injection technique will a dentist MOST commonly use for maxillary teeth?   4._____
    A. Nerve block   B. Field block
    C. Infiltration   D. Subgingival

5. The area or bump found just behind the third molar is referred to as   5._____
    A. tuberosity   B. alveolar ridge
    C. alveolar socket   D. retro molar pad

6. The band of connective tissue found next to the bicuspids and lips is referred to as   6._____
    A. labia   B. mucosa   C. frenum   D. alveolar ridge

7. Which tooth has a fifth cusp called the Cusp of Carabelli?   7._____
    A. Maxillary first molar   B. Maxillary second molar
    C. Mandibular first bicuspid   D. Mandibular first molar

8. A tofflemire and matrix band is used to form a wall on which cavity classification?   8._____
    A. Class II   B. Class III   C. Class IV   D. Class V

9. When using a rubber dam, which size hole is typically used for a first molar?   9._____
    A. 1   B. 2   C. 3   D. 4

10. If a patient takes a large amount of salicylates, which of the following is MOST likely to be affected?
    A. Sensitivity to antibiotics   B. Tolerance to pain
    C. Bleeding and clotting time   D. Tolerance to general anesthesia

10.____

11. If an error is made on a clinical record entry, what should be done to correct the error?
    A. Circle the incorrect entry in red
    B. Erase the error and rewrite the entry correctly
    C. Mark through the incorrect entry so that it cannot be read
    D. Draw one line through the incorrect entry and initial and write the correct entry below

11.____

12. When assisting during oral surgery, which of the following actions should be avoided?
    A. Flushing the area with water   B. Wiping oral tissue with gauze
    C. Blowing air to clear the socket   D. Suctioning the anesthetized area

12.____

13. Control of saliva from the parotid duct can be accomplished by placing a cotton roll in what location?
    A. In the vestibule opposite of the maxillary anterior teeth
    B. In the vestibule opposite of the maxillary second molar
    C. In the vestibule opposite of the mandibular second molar
    D. On the lingual side of the mandibular arch under the tongue

13.____

14. Which of the following conditions can occur if excess cement remains on the cervical margin after cementation of a crown?
    A. Inflammation of the interdental papillae
    B. Lateral movement of the adjacent tooth
    C. Increase occurrence of subgingival caries
    D. Fracture of the cervical margin of the preparation

14.____

15. In selecting an impression tray for a preliminary maxillary impression, the tray should extend posteriorly
    A. behind the tuberosity
    B. beyond the hamular process
    C. to the fauces
    D. to the junction of the hard and soft palates

15.____

16. Nitrous oxide analgesia is normally contraindicated for patients with
    A. hypertension   B. diabetes
    C. nasal congestion   D. a sensitive gag reflex

16.____

17. For what reason would wax be placed along the facial periphery of the maxillary impression tray?
    A. Increased comfort for the patient
    B. To assure registration of the tuberosities
    C. To achieve greater detail of the hard palate
    D. To obtain registration of the mucobuccal attachments

17.____

18. In order to achieve maximum effectiveness, when should pit and fissure sealants be placed?

18.____

    A. After placement of restorations
    B. After proximal surface becomes carious
    C. Prior to eruption of permanent dentition
    D. After eruption of entire occlusal surface

19. In which area of the dentition is plaque MOST likely to accumulate?

19.____

    A. Incisal surfaces   B. Buccal surfaces
    C. Occlusal surfaces   D. Proximal spaces

20. To ensure adequate extension of the impression when seating the mandibular impression tray for diagnostic casts, the dental assistant should instruct the patient to

20.____

    A. open mouth very wide   B. raise the mandible
    C. elevate the tongue   D. drop the chin to the chest

21. Which of the following refers to the grating sound heard in a patient with temporomandibular joint disorder?

21.____

    A. Trismus   B. Rales   C. Crepitus   D. Bruits

22. Which of the following bur/handpiece combinations would MOST often be used for removing the carious dentin from the cavity preparation?

22.____

    A. #4 bur in a low-speed handpiece
    B. #56 bur in a high-speed handpiece
    C. #330 bur in a high-speed handpiece
    D. #702 bur in a low-speed handpiece

23. When assisting a dentist using a high-speed handpiece during a tooth preparation, what is the PRIMARY purpose for using the air/water syringe?

23.____

    A. To keep the mirror clean
    B. To eliminate the need for a cuspidor
    C. To blow debris away from the operating area
    D. To keep the operating area from overheating

24. When a right-handed dentist is preparing the occlusal of tooth #14, the dental assistant is responsible for retracting what area of the patient's face?

24.____

    A. Tongue   B. Lower lip   C. Left cheek   D. Right cheek

25. What dental specialty deals with the removal of pulp?

25.____

    A. Endodontics   B. Periodontics
    C. Orthodontics   D. Prosthodontics

26. Which of the following cements possess anticariogenic properties?

26.____

    A. Zinc phosphate   B. Glass ionomer
    C. Polycarboxylate   D. Zinc oxide eugenol

27. Which of the following is the activating compound for a visible light curing system?
    A. Ubiquinone   B. Camphorquinone
    C. Hydroquinone   D. Potassium oxide
    27.____

28. What type of cement is extensively used for attachment of orthodontic brackets to teeth?
    A. Resin   B. Silicate
    C. Copper oxide   D. Glass ionomer
    28.____

29. What type of cement has antibacterial properties?
    A. Polycarboxylate   B. Zinc phosphate
    C. Copper oxide   D. Zinc oxide eugenol
    29.____

30. Which part of an amalgam restoration has the HIGHEST mercury concentration?
    A. Pulpal area   B. Marginal area
    C. Center of the restoration   D. Proximal surface of the restoration
    30.____

KEY (CORRECT ANSWERS)

1. B	11. D	21. C
2. B	12. C	22. A
3. A	13. B	23. A
4. C	14. A	24. C
5. A	15. A	25. A
6. C	16. C	26. B
7. A	17. D	27. B
8. A	18. A	28. A
9. D	19. D	29. C
10. C	20. C	30. B

FUNDAMENTALS OF DENTAL ASSISTING

SECTION 1: DIDACTIC EDUCATION: FUNDAMENTALS OF DENTAL ASSISTING

Table 1. Educational Parameters of the Didactic Component of the Fundamentals of Dental Assisting Curriculum		
Unit	**Title**	**Number of Tasks**
1	Introduction to the Dental Profession	33
2	Dentistry and the Law	56
3	Dental Terminology	191
4	Preventative Oral Health	53
5	Infection Control	200
6	Patient Management	66
7	Anatomy	80
8	Dental Equipment	50
9	Dental Instruments and Procedures	121
10	Clinical Records	84
11	Oral Pathology	68
12	Emergency Care	60
13	Dental Anesthesia	75
14	Chair-Side Assisting	66
15	Dental Materials	82
16	Introduction to Dental Radiography	190
	Total	1,475

FUNDAMENTALS OF DENTAL ASSISTING

1.0 INTRODUCTION TO THE DENTAL PROFESSION

(I) Number of Tasks to Master = 33

(II) Intended Outcome: Given information about the dental team, specialties, and dental assisting credentials, the student will perform 85% of the following tasks with accuracy on the didactic exam.

(III) Tasks:

1.01 The Dental Team

A. Identify five members of the dental profession:
1. Dentist
2. Dental Assistant
3. Dental Hygienist
4. Business Assistant
5. Dental Laboratory Technician

B. Define the five members of the dental team:
1. Dentist: Leader of the dental team, responsible for all of the treatment and care of the patient.
2. Dental Assistant: Aids the dentist in diagnosis, treatment and dental care.
3. Dental Hygienist: Concerned with the prevention of dental disease, specializing in the cleaning, polishing, and radiographing teeth, periodontal treatment, and patient education.
4. Business Assistant: Responsible for the smooth and efficient operation of the business office.
5. Dental Laboratory Technician: Performs dental lab procedures according to a written prescription of a licensed dentist.

1.02 The Dental Specialties

A. Describe the nine specialty fields of dentistry:
1. Dental Public Health: Involves public/community education to control and prevent disease.
2. Endodontics: Concerned with the cause, diagnosis, prevention, and treatment of diseases and injuries to the pulp and associated structures.
3. Oral and Maxillofacial Radiology: Enhance imaging techniques to locate tumors and infectious diseases of the jaw, assist in trauma cases, and help pinpoint temporomandibular disorders, newest of the specialties.
4. Oral and Maxillofacial Surgery: Involves the diagnosis and surgical treatment of diseases, injuries, and defects of the oral and maxillofacial regions.
5. Oral Pathology: Concerned with the nature of the diseases affecting the oral cavity and adjacent structures. Perform biopsies and work closely with oral surgeons to provide a diagnosis.
6. Orthodontics: Involves the diagnosis, prevention, interception, and treatment of all forms of malocclusion of the teeth and associated structures.

7. Pediatric Dentistry: Concerned with the oral health care of children from birth to adolescence, often dealing with emotional or behavioral problems.
8. Periodontics: Concerned with the diagnosis and treatment of the oral tissues supporting and surrounding the teeth.
9. Prosthodontics: Concerned with the restoration and replacement of natural teeth with artificial replacements.

1.03 Dental Assisting Credentials

A. Define seven acronyms for identification of dental assistants:
1. CDA: Certified Dental Assistant
2. CDPMA: Certified Dental Practice Management Administrator
3. COA: Certified Orthodontic Assistant
4. COSMA: Certified Oral and Maxillofacial Surgery Assistant
5. RDA: Registered Dental Assistant
6. RDAEF: Registered Dental Assistant in Expanded Functions
7. EFDA: Expanded Function Dental Assistant

B. Explain how each of the seven dental assisting credentials may be obtained:
1. CDA: Granted by the Dental Assisting National Board after successful completion of the national certification examination.
2. CDPMA: Granted by the Dental Assisting National Board to recognize successful completion of the specialty examination in dental practice management.
3. COA: Granted by the Dental Assisting National Board to recognize successful completion of the specialty examination on Orthodontics.
4. COMSA: This credential is no longer granted but is still recognized. Granted by the Dental Assisting National Board to recognize successful completion of a specialty examination in oral and maxillofacial surgery.
5. RDA: Given by some states to indicate that specific requirements have been met to practice expanded and advanced functions for that state.
6. RDAEF: Given by some states to indicate that specific requirements have been met to practice expanded and advanced functions in that state.
7. EFDA: Given by some states to indicate specific requirements have been met to practice expanded and advanced functions of that state.

2.0 DENTAL ETHICS AND THE LAW
(I) Number of Tasks to Master = 56
(II) Intended Outcome: Given information about legal, ethical, and risk management considerations, the student will be able to perform 85% of the following tasks on the didactic examination.
(III) Tasks:

2.01 Legal Considerations

A. Identify and give the function of five agencies that regulate dentistry:
1. State Board of Dentistry
2. Drug Enforcement Agency
3. State Board of Pharmacy
4. Occupational Safety and Health Administration
5. Environmental Protection Agency

B. Identify current prohibitions specified by Rule 35 of the Idaho Dental Practice Act.

C. Define two types of law that affect dentistry:
1. Civil Law (i.e., malpractice suit)
   a. Contract Law
   b. Tort Law
2. Criminal Law (i.e., unlicensed dentistry, fraud)

D. List who may be the subject of a lawsuit:
1. Initiating Dentist
2. Dental Assistant
3. Hygienist

E. State the purpose of professional liability insurance.

F. Explain who owns the dental record.

2.02 Ethical Considerations

A. Define ethical behavior.

B. Define five ethical concepts that are important to a dental assistant:
1. Confidentiality
2. Respect for the profession
3. Respect for fellow staff and dentist
4. Maintain skills and knowledge
5. Refrain from services prohibited by state law

2.03 Risk Management Considerations

A. Define risk management.

B. List seven elements of an informed consent:
1. Description of treatment
2. Alternatives of treatment
3. Risk of complications
4. Prognosis
5. Cost
6. Time needed to complete
7. Age and mental capacity of patient

C. Explain three ways to obtain informed consent:
1. Implied consent
2. Verbal consent
3. Written consent

D. Describe thirteen ways to manage risk:
1. Informed consent
2. Review medical history
3. Emergency preparedness
4. Clear/Realistic patient expectations
5. Maintain high level of skill
6. Adequate patient safety equipment
7. Disclosure of unexpected events
8. Comprehensive/accurate treatment record
9. Never criticize previous treatment
10. Protect privacy of patient (HIPPA)
11. Document privacy of patient (HIPPA)
12. Identify responsibility/obligations in the dentist/patient relationship
13. How to respond to a threat of malpractice suit

E. List six guidelines for managing chart entries as a legal record:
1. Keep a separate chart for each patient
2. Correct errors properly
3. Make chart entry during patient visit, do not rely on memory
4. Write legibly, in ink, date and initial each entry
5. The entry should be complete
6. Never change or alter the chart after a problem arises

3.0   DENTAL TERMINOLOGY
(I)   Number of Tasks to Master = 191
(II)   Intended Outcome: Given information about the value of dental terminology, prefixes, word roots, and suffixes, the student will perform the following tasks with 85% accuracy on the didactic examination.
(III) Tasks:

3.01   Dental Prefixes

A. List and define the following 83 dental prefixes:
1. a-; an-   without, away from, not
2. ab-   from, away negative, absent
3. ad-   increase, toward
4. an-   without, not
5. ana-   up, throughout
6. ano-   up
7. anti-   opposed to, against, counteracting
8. auto-   self
9. bi-   two, twice, double
10. bio-   life
11. brady-   slow
12. canth-   corner of the eye

13.	circum-	around
14.	contra-	against, opposed
15.	de-	from, lack of
16.	demi-	half
17.	dens-	tooth
18.	dent-	tooth, teeth
19.	derma-	skin
20.	di-	twice, double
21.	dia-	complete, through
22.	dors-	back
23.	dys-	bad, difficult, painful
24.	e-/ec-	out of, from
25.	ecto-	external, outside
26.	edem/a-	swelling
27.	endo-	within
28.	epi-	over, upper, upon
29.	erythr/o	red
30.	eth/m-	sieve
31.	eti/o	cause
32.	ex-; ex/o	out away from, completely
33.	extra-	beyond, outside
34.	faci/a	face, appearance
35.	fore-	in front of
36.	gene-	origin, beget
37.	hem/a/i	blood
38.	hepa-	liver
39.	homo-	same
40.	hydra-	water
41.	hyo-	U-shaped, horshoe-shaped
42.	hyper-	above, excessive, beyond
43.	hypo-	less than, below, under
44.	idio-	peculiar, one's own
45.	inter-	in the midst, between
46.	intra-	within
47.	infra-	beneath, under, inferior
48.	leuk/o	white
49.	macro-	large
50.	mal-	evil, sickness, disorder, bad, poor
51.	mesi/o	middle
52.	mucos/a	mucus membrane
53.	myel/o	spinal cord, bone marrow
54.	myo-	muscle
55.	neo-	new
56.	necr/a	death, dead
57.	nephr/o	kidney
58.	neuro-	nerve
59.	nutri-	feed, nourish
60.	pan-	all
61.	para-	besides, beyond
62.	peri-	around, about

63.	poly-	many, much
64.	post-	behind, after
65.	pre-	before, in front of
66.	pseudo-	false
67.	ptery-	a wing
68.	ptya/l	spit, saliva
69.	pyo-	pus
70.	re-	back, again
71.	retro-	backwards
72.	sub-	under, beneath, less normal
73.	super-	above, superior, beyond
74.	supra-	above, excessive
75.	syn-	together, union
76.	tachy-	fast
77.	tic-	relation, belonging to
78.	trans-	across, over, beyond, through
79.	tri-	three, trice, third
80.	ventro	body front
81.	ultra-	beyond, excess
82.	un-	not
83.	uni-	one

3.02 Dental Root Words

A. List and define the following 55 dental root words:

1.	alve/o	alveolus (tooth socket bone)
2.	amalg	soft mass
3.	amel/o	tooth, enamel tissue
4.	angio	vessel
5.	ankyl	anchored, crooked
6.	anter/o	before, in front of
7.	apic/o	apex of the root, tip
8.	brux/i/o	chew, grind
9.	bucc	cheek
10.	calcul	small stone, limestone
11.	cardi/o	heart
12.	carcin/o	cancer
13.	cari/es/o	rottenness, decay
14.	cephal/o	head
15.	cheil/o	lip
16.	clavi/o	a club
17.	cocci	round, spherical bacteria
18.	colli	neck
19.	coron/a	crown
20.	cyan/o	blue
21.	cyst	fluid filled sac
22.	cyt	cell
23.	decidu	shedding
24.	dens/t	tooth
25.	di	across, separate apart

26.	diastema/a	space, interval
27.	dist/o	farthest from center
28.	edem/a	swelling
29.	edentul/o	without teeth
30.	erythr/o	red
31.	fluor/o	fluoride
32.	foss/o	shallow depression
33.	frene	frenum, connecting tissue
34.	gingiv	gingival, gum tissue
35.	gloss/o	tongue
36.	halit/o	breath
37.	hem/a/o	blood
38.	incis/o	incisor tooth
39.	infer/o	under, below
40.	labi/o	lip area
41.	lacrim/o	tears
42.	lingu/o	tongue
43.	lip/i/o	fat
44.	lith/o	stone
45.	mandibul/a	lower jaw
46.	mastic/o	chew
47.	maxilla/a/o	upperjaw
48.	melan/o	black
49.	mesi/o	middle, mid-line
50.	muc/o	tissue lining an orifice
51.	my/o	muscle
52.	occlus/o	occlusion, jaw closing
53.	orth/o	straight, proper order
54.	stoma	mouth
55.	tempor/o	temporal bone/joint

3.03   Dental Suffixes

A. List and define the following 52 dental suffixes:

1.	-ac, -ic, -ar	describes or shows relation to
2.	-al	used to indicate connection with
3.	-algia/-esia	pain, suffering
4.	-ia	state of being
5.	-ase	enzyme
6.	-cife	kill
7.	-cise	cut into
8.	-cyte	cell
9.	-dema	swelling
10.	-ectomy	surgical removal
11.	--emia	blood
12.	-eme/-tic/-sis	producing vomiting
13.	-esthesia	sensation
14.	-eum	a place where
15.	-graph/y	picture, recording of a picture
16.	-gram	graph, picture (used in radiology)

17.	-iama	medicine, remedy
18.	-iasis	abnormal condition
19.	-im	not, in, into
20.	-ism	state of, condition
21.	-ist	specialist in, superlative
22.	-it is	inflammation of
23.	-ium	small
24.	-ize	take away, remove
25.	-lar	describing, about
26.	-lith	stone
27.	-logist	specialist
28.	-logy	study of
29.	-lysis	destruction
30.	-nomy	science of
31.	-oid	like, resembling
32.	-ology	study of
33.	-oma	tumor, swelling
34.	-orrhea	flow, excessive flow
35.	-otomy	cutting into, incision into
36.	-osis	abnormal, condition of
37.	-ous	pertaining to, full of
38.	-path/o/y	disease
39.	-phob	fear, dread
40.	-plasty	surgical correction
41.	-pnea	breathing
42.	-rrhage	excessive flow
43.	-rrhea	excessive
44.	-scoli/o	twisted
45.	-scopy	scan, visual exam
46.	-sis	the act of
47.	-stalsis	constriction, contraction
48.	-tic	pertaining to
49.	-tome	cutting instrument
50.	-trophy	development, growth, nourishment
51.	-um	pertaining to
52.	-y	act, result of an act

4.0   PREVENTIVE ORAL HEALTH

(I)   Number of Tasks to Master = 53

(II)   Intended Outcome: Given information about preventive dentistry, plaque removal, fluoride, and nutrition, the student will be able to perform the following tasks with 85% accuracy on the didactic examination.

(III)   Tasks:

4.01   Comprehensive Preventive Dentistry

A. Explain the goal of preventive dentistry.

B. Describe the five parts of a comprehensive preventive dentistry program:
   1. Nutrition
   2. Patient education
   3. Plaque control
   4. Fluoride therapy
   5. Sealants

4.02 Bacterial Plaque

A. Explain the composition of plaque.

B. Explain the three steps of plaque formation:
   1. Pellicle formation nutrition
   2. Bacteria attach to the pellicle
   3. Bacteria multiply and mature

4.03 Dental Calculus

A. Define dental calculus:
   1. Dental calculus is mineralized bacterial plaque. It is a tenacious deposit that forms on the clinical crowns and roots of teeth.

B. List the two types of dental calculus:
   1. Supragingival calculus
   2. Subgingival calculus

4.04 Dental Caries

A. Explain the five stages that must be present for the development of caries:
   1. Cariogenic food, in the form of carbohydrates, are mixed in with the plaque.
   2. Plaque and bacteria mix together and the pH of the plaque becomes more acidic.
   3. Acid formation begins.
   4. Frequent exposure of tooth to acid begins demineralization of the tooth structure.
   5. Caries formation.

B. Define cariogenic:
   1. Producing or promoting tooth decay.

C. List two factors that contribute to dental caries:
   1. A diet high in cariogenic foods
   2. Frequent exposure to sucrose

4.05 Periodontal Disease

A. List the main contributing factor in periodontal disease:
   1. Bacterial plaque

B. List four contributing factors in periodontal disease:
1. Inadequate plaque control
2. Lack of patient compliance
3. Tobacco use
4. Systemic diseases

4.06 Patient Education

A. Evaluation of patient:
1. Oral health status and habits
2. Use appropriate disclosing aids
3. Provide individualized education plan
4. Evaluate patients' progress

B. List four factors in toothbrush selection:
1. Soft bristles
2. Easily cleaned
3. Replaceable every 3-4-months
4. Adapted to individual patient

C. Describe two toothbrushing techniques:
1. Bass or sulcular brushing technique
2. Rolling or circular brushing technique

D. List three flossing considerations:
1. Floss every 24 hours
2. Most effectively removes plaque between teeth
3. Choice of type depends on individual patient needs

E. Describe five special interdental aids:
1. Floss holder
2. Floss threader
3. Stimulators
4. Interproximal brush
5. Oral irrigation device

4.07 Fluoride

A. Describe two methods of fluoride delivery, advantages, and disadvantages:
1. Types of systemic
2. Types of topical

B. Explain the possible dangers of fluoride:
1. Define dental fluorosis
2. Overdose

4.08 Nutrition

A. Define cariogenic foods.

B. Describe three effects cariogenic foods have on dental health:
1. Promotes plaque formation
2. Promotes tooth decay
3. Promotes periodontal disease

C. Provide dietary assessment related to dental health.

5.0 INFECTION CONTROL

(I) Number of Tasks to Master = 200
(II) Intended Outcome: Given information about disease transmission, infectious diseases, universal precautions, the treatment room, cleaning, sterilization, disinfecting, disinfectants, hazards, and instrument sterilization, the student will be able to perform the following tasks with 85% accuracy on the didactic examination.
(III) Tasks:

5.01 Disease Transmission

A. Define pathogenic:
1. Disease causing microorganisms

B. Define spore:
1. Highly resistant form of bacteria that are able to remain inactive under unfavorable conditions and can become active when conditions are favorable.

C. Define five modes of disease transmission in a dental office:
1. Direct transmission
2. Indirect transmission
3. Splatter or splash
4. Airborne transmission
5. Dental water lines

D. List and explain three methods for airborne transmission:
1. Splatter: Large particles, such as tooth fragments and debris are released into the air during cavity preparations.
2. Mists: Droplets transported via coughing causing respiratory infections.
3. Aerosols: Microorganisms are found in the aerosols created by ultrasonic scalers, high-speed handpieces, and the use of air-water syringes.

E. Define cross-examination:
1. Cross-contamination refers to the spread of microorganisms from one source to another source.

F. List two methods in which cross-contamination can occur:
1. Person-to-person contact
2. Person to an inanimate object, and then to another person

G. List three ways to prevent cross-contamination:
   1. Reduction of pathogenic microorganisms
   2. Breaking the chain of disease transmission
   3. Application of universal precautions

5.02 Infectious Diseases

A. List and explain the five types of hepatitis and the route of transmission for each type:
   1. Hepatitis 1: Fecal and oral
   2. Hepatitis B (HBV): Blood, saliva, and body fluids
   3. Hepatitis C: Percutaneous, blood, and contaminated needles
   4. Hepatitis D (Delta): Co-infection with hepatitis B, blood, sexual contact, and perinatal
   5. Hepatitis E: Fecal and oral, contaminated water

B. Explain five types of individuals at risk for contracting hepatitis B:
   1. Patients with active or chronic liver disease
   2. Military populations stationed in countries with a high incidence of hepatitis B
   3. Infants born to HIV-infected mothers
   4. IV drug users
   5. Heterosexually active persons with multiple sexual partners

C. Explain the time interval for administering the hepatitis B vaccine:
   1. Administered in three doses: initial dose and then at one and six months

D. List two types of herpes viruses:
   1. Herpes simplex virus-1
   2. Herpes simplex virus-2

E. List three reasons to postpone treatment for a patient with an active herpetic lesion:
   1. Contiguousness of the lesion
   2. Transfer of the virus to other areas of the face
   3. Irritation to the lesion from dental procedures can prolong healing

F. Define the term HIV
   1. Human immunodeficiency virus

G. List and explain three modes of transmission for HIV:
   1. Perinatal: Transmission across the placenta, during delivery, or breast-feeding
   2. Sexual Contact: Heterosexual or homosexual relations
   3. IV Drug Users: Shared or contaminated needles

H. List four other diseases of concern to dental health workers:
   1. Tuberculosis
   2. Tetanus
   3. Legionnaires'
   4. Measles

5.03   Prevention of Disease Transmission

A. Define the four factors of disease transmission
   1. Virulence
   2. Pathogenic organisms must be present in quantities and concentration sufficient to overtake the body defenses
   3. A susceptible host must be present, one who cannot resist infection
   4. Pathogens must have means of entering the body (portal of entry)

B. Explain eight methods used to prevent disease transmission:
   1. Eliminating or controlling the organisms found in the oral cavity by brushing teeth or rinsing with an antiseptic mouthwash
   2. Interruption of transmission of organisms by the use of rubber dam and high-speed evacuation system
   3. Wearing protective eyewear, gloves and mask (universal precautions)
   4. Sterilization of dental instruments by autoclaving
   5. Use of disposables when possible
   6. Immunization of dental personnel
   7. Avoid procedures on patients with lesions of communicable diseases
   8. Properly store all instruments and materials

5.04   OSHA Bloodborne Pathogens Standard

A. List the components required by the OSHA Bloodborne Pathogen Standards:
   1. Exposure control plan
   2. Standard and Universal Precaution
   3. Categorization of employees
   4. Post exposure management
   5. Employee training
   6. Hepatitis B immunization

B. List OSHA Bloodborne Pathogens Standard Training Requirements:
   1. Epidemiology, modes of transmission, and prevention of HBV and HIV
   2. Risks to the fetus from HBV and HIV
   3. Location and proper use of all protective equipment
   4. Proper work practices using Universal Precautions
   5. Meaning of color codes, biohazard symbol, and precautions to following handling infectious waste
   6. Procedures to follow if needlestick or other injury occurs

C. Management of an Exposure Incident:
   1. Document routes of exposure
   2. Document source
   3. Request blood screening of source

4. Advise employee to be tested
5. Provide prophylaxis treatment
6. Provide appropriate counseling
7. Evaluate post incident illness

5.05   Universal Precaution

A. Define universal precautions:
1. The same infection control procedure for any dental procedure must be used for ALL patients. All human blood and body fluids are treated as contaminated.

B. List and explain seven appropriate personal protective guidelines:
1. Uniform tops should be closed at the neck, disposable or easily laundered and have long sleeves with fitted cuffs. Pants and socks should cover the legs and ankles.
2. Clinic attire must not be worn in the staff lounge or outside the dental office. Clothing must be changed daily.
3. Hair should be worn off the shoulders and away from the face. Facial hair should be covered with a face mask or shield.
4. Face masks must have a high bacterial infiltration efficiency rate. Masks should be changed after each patient or after becoming splattered and/or saturated.
5. Protective eyewear should have wide side shields to protect the area around the eyes, and shatterproof lenses that are made of sturdy plastic.
6. Gloves should be impermeable to saliva, blood, and bacteria and fit snug over the cuffs of the uniform.
7. Other barrier items such as dental dams.

C. Describe the six guidelines for use of gloves:
1. Gloves must be worn by all dental staff during the patient's treatment.
2. Torn or damaged gloves must be replaced immediately.
3. Do not wear jewelry under gloves.
4. Change gloves frequently, with each new patient or approximately every hour.
5. Contaminated gloves should be removed before leaving the operatory during patient treatment.
6. Hands must be washed after glove removal and before re-gloving.

D. List three types of gloves worn:
1. Overgloves
2. Utility gloves
3. Non-sterile latex or non-latex

E. List three principles of effective handwashing:
1. Reduction of the bacterial flora on the skin
2. Removal of surface dirt and loosened debris
3. Provide disinfection with a long-acting antiseptic

F. List the seven steps for washing and drying of hands:
   1. Remove all jewelry.
   2. Wet hands with warm water.
   3. Apply an ample amount of antibacterial liquid soap.
   4. Vigorously rub hands together under a stream of water.
   5. Rub together for a minimum of 15 seconds.
   6. Rinse hands with cool water.
   7. Using a paper towel, thoroughly dry your hands.

G. State three guidelines for handling contaminated laundry:
   1. Protective clothing should be laundered in the office and universal precautions are followed when handling the clothing.
   2. Disposable gowns are discarded daily, more often if visibly soiled.
   3. Contaminated clothing that is removed from the office must be in a leak-proof bag that is labeled "Biohazard."

5.06   Management of Hazardous Materials

A. List three organizations that regulate the profession of dentistry:
   1. Occupational Safety and Health Administration (OSHA)
   2. Centers for Disease Control (CDC)
   3. Environmental Protection Agency (EPA)

B. Define four classifications of waste:
   1. General waste
   2. Hazardous waste
   3. Contaminated waste
   4. Infectious or regulated waste

C. List four methods for disposal of waste:
   1. Gloves, mask, and barriers contaminated with body fluids or blood should be discarded in impermeable plastic bags as general waste.
   2. Sharps should be placed in a puncture-resistant, leakproof container and labeled as biohazard.
   3. Blood, blood-soaked materials, tissue and teeth should be placed in leakproof containers, labeled biohazard and disposed of according to state guidelines for infectious waste.
   4. Proper disposal of liquid chemicals or solid chemicals may vary with local and state waste management agencies. Check with the local agencies in your area.

D. Explain the five parts of the OSHA hazard communication standard:
   1. Written
   2. Chemical inventory
   3. MSDS sheets
   4. Container labeling
   5. Employee training

E. General protection against chemical hazards:
1. Hand and eye protection
2. Ventilation
3. Handling and storage
4. Disposal

5.07 Cleaning/Pre-cleaning

A. Define cleaning/pre-cleaning:
1. Initial removal of debris and reduction of bioburden

B. List three appropriate methods for cleaning instruments prior to sterilization:
1. Ultrasonic cleaning
2. Soaking instruments in a disinfectant solution
3. Automatic washers

C. Explain three advantages of an ultrasonic cleaner:
1. Reduced risk to operator from contact with contaminated instruments
2. Penetration into difficult areas of instruments where brushes cannot reach
3. Improved effectiveness in removing debris and blood from instruments

D. List the four steps for cleaning instruments manually:
1. Wear heavy duty gloves, mask, and protective eyewear. Dismantle instruments if parts are detachable.
2. Use detergent and scrub instruments with a brush under running water.
3. Brush away from the body and avoid splashing the surrounding area.
4. Rinse instruments thoroughly and dry on paper towels.

5.08 Disinfection

A. Define disinfection:
1. Killing or inhibiting pathogens by chemical means. Spores are not killed by disinfection.

B. Define the term disinfectant:
1. Chemicals that are applied to inanimate objects (countertops) that cannot be sterilized.

C. State the three types of disinfectants and their biocidal activity:
1. High Level: Inactivates all forms of bacteria, fungi, spores, and viruses.
2. Intermediate Level: Inactivates all forms of microorganisms except spores.
3. Low Level: Inactivates vegetative bacteria and certain viruses, but does not destroy spores, tubercle bacilli or non-lipid viruses.

D. List five properties of an ideal disinfectant:
1. Broad spectrum
2. Nontoxic
3. Easy to use

4. Fast acting
5. Economical

E. Explain the four recommended chemical disinfectants:
1. Chlorines: Sodium hypochlorite is unstable, use distilled water to improve stability. Economical, harmful to the eyes and skin.
2. Glutaraldehydes: Solution is activated when the two containers are mixed. Not used as a surface disinfectant, toxic fumes. Caustic to skin and eye.
3. Iodophores: Broad spectrum antimicrobial, hard water inactivates iodophores. Widely used for surgical scrubs, liquid soaps.
4. Combination Phenolics: Used as surface disinfectants. Broad spectrum with residual biocidal activity.

5.09 Sterilization

A. Define sterilization:
1. A process (usually by heat) by which all forms of life (including spores) are completely destroyed.

B. Explain the four approved methods for sterilization:
1. Moist Heat (or steam under pressure): Sterilization is achieved by the action of heat and moisture. Pressure is used to reach high temperatures.
2. Dry Heat: Sterilization is achieved by heat conducted from the exterior surface to the interior of the object.
3. Chemical Vapor Steam: A combination of chemicals is heated under pressure which produces a gas-sterilizing agent.
4. Ethylene Oxide: Commonly used in hospitals. Gaseous sterilization using ethylene oxide.

C. List two items that can be sterilized using dry heat:
1. Metal instruments in containers
2. Instruments that may corrode or rust if exposed to moisture

D. Explain two advantages for using steam under pressure:
1. All spores, microorganisms, and viruses are destroyed quickly.
2. Economical method for sterilizing instruments.

E. List the temperatures for dry heat, steam under pressure, and chemical vapor:
1. Dry Heat: 320°F for two hours; 340°F for one hour
2. Steam Under Pressure: 250°F at 15 pounds of pressure for 15 minutes; 30 minutes for heavy or large loads
3. Chemical Vapor: 260° to 270°F at 20 to 40 pounds of pressure. Minimum of 20 minutes after the desired temperature and pressure is reached.

F. List two reasons for spore testing:
1. To ensure proper sterilization
2. To verify proper function of the sterilizer

G. Explain the frequency of spore testing:
   1. Weekly testing is recommended.

H. Explain heat process monitoring

5.10 Instrument Processing

A. List the seven steps for instrument processing:
   1. Transport
   2. Cleaning
   3. Packaging
   4. Sterilization
   5. Storage
   6. Delivery
   7. Quality assurance

5.11 Treatment Room

A. List six features of an optimal treatment room:
   1. Floor covering is easy to clean. No carpeting.
   2. Stools and dental chairs have a smooth surface that is easily disinfected.
   3. Water faucets should be electronic or foot-operated.
   4. Dental chairs are foot-operated.
   5. Hoses are straight and removable.
   6. Syringes and handpieces are autoclavable

B. List four objects that require barrier protection:
   1. Dental light handles
   2. Head rest and dental chair
   3. Air/water syringe
   4. Saliva ejector and HVE handles

C. Explain the classification of surface categories for inanimate objects:
   1. Critical: Penetrates soft tissue or bone. Example: Needles, dental instruments. *Sterilize or dispose.*
   2. Semi-Critical: Touch intact mucous membranes and oral fluids but does not penetrate. Example: Ultrasonic handpiece, probe. *Sterilize or high level disinfectant.*
   3. Non-Critical: Does not touch mucous membranes. *Intermediate level of disinfection.*
   4. Environmental Surfaces: No contact with patient. *Intermediate to low level disinfection.*

D. List six steps in cleaning and preparing the treatment room:
   1. Wear heavy-duty gloves and mask.
   2. Flush handpieces.
   3. Select appropriate disinfectant and prepare according to manufacturer.
   4. Clean the surfaces with gauze soaked in a precleaning/disinfectant.

5.   Scrub the disinfectant over the surface.

6.   Wipe with disinfectant and leave the surfaces wet for manufacturers recommended time.

5.12   Dental Unit Water Lines

A. List five features of an optimal treatment room:
1. Use water that meets EPA standards for drinking water.
2. Consult dental manufacturer for methods to maintain quality of water.
3. Follow manufacturer recommendations for monitoring quality of water.
4. After each patient discharge air/water 20-30 seconds.
5. Follow manufacturer recommendations for maintenance schedule.

B. Methods to reduce bacterial contamination of dental unit waterlines:
1. Flush water lines for several minutes each morning.
2. Use self-contained water system.
3. Use periodic or continuous chemical germicides.
4. Use sterile water for surgery.
5. Purge water from surgery lines at end of day.
6. Use microfilm cartridges.
7. Use current techniques and technology.
8. Follow manufacturer recommendations.

6.0   PATIENT MANAGEMENT

(I)   Number of Tasks to Master = 66

(II)   Intended Outcome: Given information about utilizing effective communication skills, non-verbal communication, obtaining information and managing patient behavior the student will be able to answer 85% of the questions on the didactic exam.

(III) Tasks:

6.01   Utilizing Effective Communication Skills

A. List 10 alternative terms to use in effective communication:
1. Pull a tooth/remove a tooth
2. Shot, needle/injection
3. Pain, hurt/discomfort
4. Plates, false teeth/dentures
5. Spit/rinse your mouth
6. Drugs/medication
7. Filling/restoration
8. Drill/prepare or handpiece
9. Yeah/yes
10. Cap/crown

B. List three rules of etiquette:
1. Do not use nicknames or terms of endearment in an office setting.
2. Compliment and praise.
3. Avoid the subjects of politics, religion, gender, ethnic, and off-color jokes.

6.02 Non-Verbal Communication

A. Identify four key steps for improving telephone communications:
1. Smile.
2. Identify the office, yourself, and ask, "How may I help you?"
3. Listen and be attentive.
4. Take notes.

B. Describe seven items important to non-verbal communication:
1. Good grooming versus bad grooming.
2. Professional hair styles.
3. The use of fragrances and deodorants.
4. The appearance of hands and nails.
5. The effect of oral hygiene.
6. Professional attire.
7. Make-up.

C. Identify two effects of body language and posture:
1. Slouching
2. Crossed arms

D. List two examples of patient non-verbal cues:
1. Facial expressions
2. Body language

6.03 Greet the Patient

A. List eight items included in welcoming the patient as a guest:
1. Greet within 30 seconds.
2. Survey the reception area.
3. Sign in log.
4. Review the schedule.
5. Initiate the patient orientation.
6. Establish a relationship.
7. Use the patient's name.
8. Take notes.

B. List two areas of common courtesy and office etiquette that should be used when talking on the phone:
1. Common courtesy
2. Say please and thank you

C. Describe three steps in introductions:
1. Introduce self.
2. Identify others by name and title.
3. Maintain a schedule.

6.04 Obtaining Information

A. List two steps in obtaining information from a telephone call:
1. Record all information on chart.
2. Record information in ink and initial.

B. List two patient forms to be completed by the patient before treatment:
1. Patient registration
2. Medical/dental history

6.05 Managing Patient Behavior

A. Identify six patient rights:
1. To be treated without discrimination.
2. To be informed about treatment.
3. To be informed about fees
4. To have confidentiality.
5. To be taught how to maintain dental health.
6. To refuse treatment.

B. Describe two ways to comfort the *anxious* patient:
1. Validate feelings.
2. Accommodate patients' concerns.

C. Define the difference between *anxious* and the *phobic* patient:
1. Anxious: normal with enhanced feelings of concern.
2. Phobic: irrational fears.

D. List two methods of treating the phobic patient:
1. Behavior modification.
2. Hospital dentistry—general anesthesia.

E. List five steps to diffuse patient anger:
1. Let the patient release anger.
2. Do not second-guess.
3. Do not respond until the patient has fully vented.
4. Use the three F's: Feel, Felt, Found.
5. Avoid the urge to argue.

F. Identify four special patient management situations:
1. Elderly
2. Children
3. Pregnant
4. Mentally/physically challenged

7.0 ANATOMY
(I) Number of Tasks to Master = 80
(II) Intended Outcome: Given information about head and neck anatomy, oral anatomy, and dental anatomy, the student will be able to perform 85% of the following tasks with accuracy on the didactic examination.

(III) Tasks:

7.01 Head and Neck Anatomy

A. Locate and mark five bones or bony areas of the face and skull on the model or diagraph provided:
1. Calvarium (frontal, parietal, occipital bones)
2. Zygoma
3. Maxilla
4. Mandible
5. Nasal bones

B. Locate seven landmarks of the skull on the diagram or model provided:
1. External auditory meatus
2. Nasal fossae
3. Orbits of the eye
4. Styloid process
5. Mental foramen
6. Mandibular foramen
7. TMJ—temporal mandibular joint

C. Locate four sinuses on the model or diagram provided:
1. Maxillary
2. Ethmoid air cells
3. Frontal
4. Sphenoid

D. Locate and mark eight muscles of mastication and facial expression:
1. Buccinator
2. External pterygoid
3. Internal pterygoid
4. Masseter
5. Mentalis
6. Orbicularis oris
7. Temporal
8. Zygomatic major

E. Identify the nerves that supply the oral cavity:
1. Maxillary
2. Nasopalatine
3. Anterior palatine
4. Anterior superior alveolar
5. Middle superior alveolar
6. Posterior superior alveolar
7. Buccal
8. Mandibular
9. Lingual
10. Mental
11. Incisive

7.02 Oral Anatomy

A. Locate and label 18 structures of the oral cavity:
1. Maxillary arch
2. Mandibular arch
3. Lips
4. Mucosa, buccal or labial
5. The dental alveolus
6. Gingiva, attached and free
7. Floor of the mouth
8. Hard palate
9. Soft palate
10. Tongue
11. Tonsillar pillars
12. Tonsils
13. Pharyngeal walls
14. Retromolar pad
15. Maxillary tuberosity
16. Vestibules, buccal or labial
17. Frenum
18. Teeth

B. Locate three of the main salivary glands:
1. Parotid gland
2. Sublingual gland
3. Submandibular gland

C. Locate and label three structures of the gingiva:
1. Gingival sulcus
2. Gingival papilla
3. Gingival margin

7.03 Dental Anatomy

A. Define the following six dental anatomy terms:
1. Primary dentition
2. Permanent dentition
3. Mixed dentition
4. Contact
5. Contour
6. Occlusion

B. Identify the four kinds of teeth.

C. Locate and label the three parts of a tooth:
1. Crown
2. Root
3. Neck

D. Locate and label five tissues of a tooth:
1. Enamel
2. Dentin
3. Pulp
4. Cementum
5. Periodontal ligament

E. Locate and label the six maxillary anterior teeth:
1. Maxillary central incisors (2)
2. Maxillary lateral incisors (2)
3. Maxillary canines (2)

F. Locate and identify the 10 maxillary posterior teeth:
1. Maxillary first premolar (2)
2. Maxillary second premolar (2)
3. Maxillary first molar (2)
4. Maxillary second molar (2)
5. Maxillary third molar (2)

G. Locate and identify the six mandibular anterior teeth:
1. Mandibular central incisors (2)
2. Mandibular lateral incisors (2)
3. Mandibular canine (2)

H. Locate and identify the 10 mandibular anterior teeth:
1. Mandibular first premolar (2)
2. Mandibular second premolar (2)
3. Mandibular first molar (2)
4. Mandibular second molar (2)
5. Mandibular third molar (2)

I. Locate the six surfaces of a tooth:
1. Mesial
2. Occlusal
3. Distal
4. Buccal
5. Lingual
6. Facial

8.0 DENTAL EQUIPMENT
(I) Number of Tasks to Master = 50
(II) Intended Outcome: Given information about equipment identification and equipment uses, the student will be able to perform 85% of the following tasks necessary information, instruction, and equipment the student will be able to perform 85% of the following tasks with accuracy on the didactic examination.
(III) Tasks:

8.01 Equipment Identification

A. Describe five pieces of lab equipment:
1. Lathe
2. Handpiece/lab engine
3. Model trimmer
4. Vacuum adapter "The Machine"
5. Vibrator

B. Describe 12 pieces of equipment found in the treatment room:
1. Patient chair
2. Stools: Doctor and assistant (show footrest, indicate differences)
3. Treatment light
4. Cart/console
5. Handpieces (high speed/low speed)
6. High velocity evacuation (HVE)
7. Saliva ejector
8. Curing light
9. Air-water syringe
10. Rheostat/foot control
11. Computer
12. Amalgamator/triturator

C. Describe three items found in the sterile area:
1. Ultrasonic instrument cleaner
2. Cold disinfectant/sterilant container
3. Autoclaves/sterilization equipment

D. Describe five items in the radiographic area:
1. Control panel
2. Conventional or intraoral x-ray head
3. Lead apron-thyroid x-ray head
4. Automatic processor-daylight
5. Extraoral equipment

8.02 Equipment Uses

A. Give the uses of five lab equipment items:
1. Lathe: Polishes and grinds appliances.
2. Handpiece/Lab Engine: Trims and smooths smaller items outside the mouth.
3. Model Trimmer: Trims plaster and stone models.
4. Vacuum Adapter: Heats and adapts a variety of plastics to models, i.e., bleaching trays, mouth guards.
5. Vibrator: Used in pouring models to remove bubbles from mix and aid in pouring.

B. Give the uses of 12 treatment room items of equipment:
1. Patient Chair: Provides support and supine-seating for the patient.

2. Stools—Doctor Stool: Provides adjustable seating for the operator while performing dental treatment.
   Assistant Stool: Provides adjustable seating for the assistant while assisting in dental treatment.
3. Treatment Light: Provides illumination during dental treatment.
4. Cart/Console: Provides support supplies and easy access to equipment.
5. Handpieces: Rotary instruments that are used intraorally to cut and polish. (See dental instruments.)
6. High Velocity Evacuation: Assistant-controlled device that removes fluids and reduces aerosols. (Show tips.)
7. Saliva Ejector: Low volume device for removal oral fluids. (Show tips.)
8. Curing Light: Sets selected acrylic materials.
9. Air/Water Syringe: Provides air/water spray.
10. Rheostat-foot Control: Controls the rotary handpieces.
11. Computer: Used chairside to record and transmit data.
12. Amalgamator/Triturator: Mixes amalgam filling material.

C. Give the uses for three sterile area items:
1. Ultrasonic Instrument Cleaner: Removes debris from contaminated instruments.
2. Cold Disinfectant/Sterilant Container: Liquid for non-autoclavable items.
3. Autoclaves/Sterilization Equipment: Sterilizes equipment and instruments.

D. Give the uses of five pieces of radiographic equipment:
1. Control Panel: Controls x-ray production.
2. Conventional or Intraoral X-ray Head: Produces and directs x-rays.
3. Lead Apron: Provides patient protection during radiographs.
4. Automatic Processor: Processes x-ray film.
5. Extraoral X-ray Equipment: Takes x-rays outside the mouth.

9.0   DENTAL INSTRUMENTS AND PROCEDURES
(I)   Number of Tasks to Master = 121
(II) Intended Outcome: Given information about hand/rotary instruments and dental procedures, the student will be able to perform 85% of the following tasks with accuracy on the didactic examination.
(III) Tasks:

9.01   Hand Instruments

A. Define the term "Hand Instrument".

B. Describe four components of hand instruments:
1. Handle/shaft
2. Shank
3. Blade
4. Double-ended instruments

C. Describe six basic tray set-up instruments:
1. Mouth mirror
2. Explorer
3. Cotton pliers
4. Saliva ejector/high-volume evacuator
5. 3-way syringe tip
6. 2 x 2

D. Describe 17 restorative instruments:
1. Excavator/Spoon excavator
2. Discoid-cleoid carver
3. Hollenback carver
4. Amalgam well
5. Amalgam carrier
6. Amalgam condenser/plugger
7. Plastic composite instrument
8. Burnisher
9. Mixing spatula
10. Matrix band
11. Tofflemire/matrix retainer
12. Wedge
13. Articulating paper
14. Articulating paper forceps
15. Cord packer
16. Hand cutting instruments
17. Decay locator

E. Describe six instruments of a rubber dam procedure:
1. Dental dam material
2. Dental dam frame
3. Dental dam hole punch
4. Dental dam clamp forceps
5. Dental dam clamps
6. Floss

F. Discuss five periodontal instruments:
1. Periodontal probe
2. Curette
3. Slimline ultrasonic scaler
4. Scalers
5. Periodontal knives

G. Describe 15 endodontic instruments:
1. Gates glidden
2. Barbed broach
3. Endodontic files
4. Endodontic syringe
5. Paper points
6. Gutta-percha
7. Lentulo spirals

8. Endodontic spreader
9. Endodontic explorer
10. Endodontic condenser
11. Endodontic excavator
12. Millimeter measure
13. Rubber stoppers
14. Pulp tester
15. Apex locator

H. Describe 16 oral surgery instruments:
1. Elevator
2. Forceps
3. Surgical curette
4. Rongeur
5. Bone file
6. Bard-Parker handle
7. Blade
8. Hemostat
9. Needle holder
10. Surgical scissors
11. Tissue retractors
12. Surgical aspirator
13. Sutures
14. Bite blocks/mouth prop
15. Surgical chisel and mallet
16. Surgical handpiece/burs

9.02 Rotary Instruments

A. Describe five uses of rotary instruments:
1. Cavity preparations
2. Removing defective restorations
3. Crown preparations
4. Polishing teeth
5. Polishing and finishing restorations

B. Describe three parts of a dental bur:
1. Shank
2. Neck
3. Head

C. Identify three types of dental burs:
1. Carbide
2. Diamond stones
3. Steel burs

D. Discuss eight sizes and shapes of bur heads:
1. Round
2. Inverted cone
3. Fissures

4. Points
5. Stones
6. Mandrel
7. Rubber wheel
8. Rubber cup

E. Describe four styles of dental handpieces:
1. High-speed
2. Straight low-speed
    a. Contra-angle
    b. Prophy-angle

F. Discuss handpiece placement and removal.

G. Describe dental handpiece maintenance.

H. Discuss dental handpiece sterilization techniques.

9.03   Dental Procedures

A. List eight common dental procedures:
1. Exam
2. Prophylaxis, non-surgical periodontal therapy
3. Amalgam
4. Composite
5. Simple extraction
6. Endodontic
7. Crown and bridge preparation
8. Crown and bridge cementation

B. List tray armamentarium (tray setup):
1. Exam
2. Prophylaxis, non-surgical periodontal therapy
3. Amalgam restorations
4. Composite restorations
5. Extractions
6. Surgical procedures
7. Dental dam
8. Endodontic therapy
9. Crown and bridge preparation
10. Crown and bridge cementation
11. Anesthetics
12. Bleaching
13. Desensitization of the teeth
14. Removable prosthodontics
15. Preventive procedures
16. Impressions
17. Orthodontics
18. Occlusal adjustments

10.0   CLINICAL RECORDS
(I)   Number of Tasks to Master = 84
(II)   Intended Outcome: Given information about medical/dental histories, recording dental treatment, and dental/radiographic chartings, the student will be able to perform 85% of the following tasks on the didactic examination.
(III)   Tasks:

10.01   Medical History

A.   List six purposes for obtaining a medical history from every patient:
   1.   Provides information relevant to the etiology and diagnosis of oral conditions.
   2.   Used in treatment planning.
   3.   Reveals conditions, diseases, and drug therapy or reactions that may change treatment.
   4.   Provides insight into the emotional and/or psychological factors and attitudes that may affect patient care.
   5.   Provides baseline documentation for comparison at future appointments.
   6.   Provides a basis for legal evidence should treatment ever be called into question.

B.   Describe six conditions that may limit the ability of dental personnel together required information when answering questions:
   1.   Some patients either cannot, or choose not, to provide correct information when answering questions.
   2.   Language barriers or comprehension may limit the information obtained.
   3.   If there is a lack of privacy where the information is requested, the patient may be less than honest.
   4.   If the patient does not see the relevance between certain diseases or conditions and dental treatment, information may be withheld.
   5.   Medical conditions may be embarrassing to report.
   6.   The patient may be fearful of having dental treatment refused.

C.   List five factors that must be explained to the patient:
   1.   The need for obtaining and keeping an up-to-date medical history.
   2.   Assurance that the information obtained will be kept in strict confidence.
   3.   The relationship between general health and oral health.
   4.   The relationship between medical health and dental care.
   5.   The importance of following instructions on pre-medications, preventive dental care, and regular medical and dental care.

D.   List the five components of the medical history that must be verified:
   1.   Recordings must be made in ink.
   2.   Accuracy of all dates.
   3.   Confirm all information.
   4.   Medical alert codes.
   5.   Patient signature verifying accuracy of all information.

10.02 Dental History

A. List eight components of the dental history required:
1. Any immediate problem, discomfort, or pair reported by the patient.
2. Information about previous restorative, preventive, and specialty dental care.
3. Attitudes regarding oral health.
4. Information about personal daily oral care.
5. Anesthetic history.
6. Medical and dental radiation history and current medications.
7. History of oral or facial injuries, past medical and dental procedures.
8. Oral habits.

10.03 Dental Charting and the Dental Exam

A. List the five parts of the dental exam:
1. Radiographs
2. Diagnostic models
3. Oral examination
4. Periodontal examination
5. Examination of the teeth

B. State six purposes of the dental charting:
1. Provides a graphic representation of existing conditions.
2. An assessment tool used to develop a patient treatment plan.
3. Used during treatment to guide procedures performed.
4. Evaluate treatment by comparing initial data with follow-up findings.
5. Provides realistic evidence for legal documentation.
6. Used in forensic investigations and/or identification.

C. Define Black's classification of cavities:
1. Class I
2. Class II
3. Class III
4. Class IV
5. Class V
5. Class VI

D. Describe two types of tooth diagrams.
1. Anatomical
2. Geometric

E. Describe the Universal numbering system for teeth:
1. Universal
2. Palmer
3. FDI/ISO

F. Chart seven dental conditions that are evaluated clinically by the dentist or dental hygienist and recorded on the dental chart:
    1. Missing teeth
    2. Teeth indicated for extraction
    3. Occlusal caries
    4. Malpositioned teeth
    5. Existing restorations (amalgam, composite, gold)
    6. Sealants
    7. Appliances

G. Chart 11 dental conditions to be charted from radiographs:
    1. Missing teeth
    2. Unerupted teeth
    3. Impacted teeth
    4. Endodontic restorations
    5. Periapical abscesses
    6. Retained primary teeth
    7. Retained root tips
    8. Proximal carious lesions
    9. Recurrent carious lesions
    10. Bone loss
    11. Other deviations from normal

H. State six tooth surfaces where periodontal pocket readings are recorded on the periodontal chart:
    1. Distofacial
    2. Facial
    3. Mesiofacial
    4. Distolingual
    5. Lingual
    6. Mesiolingual

10.04 Recording Dental Treatment

A. Record all pertinent information:
    1. Record in ink
    2. One entry per line
    3. Anesthetic used
    4. Tooth treated
    5. Types of materials used
    6. Clear and concise
    7. Sign/Initial and date
    8. Proper correction methods

11.0 ORAL PATHOLOGY
(I)   Number of Tasks to Master = 68
(II)   Intended Outcome: Given information about dental caries; attrition, abrasion, and soft tissue pathology, the student will be able to perform 85% of the following tasks with accuracy on the didactic examination.
(III) Tasks:

11.01 Dental Caries

A. Define caries:
1. An abnormal condition of a tooth or bone characterized by decay, disintegration and destruction of the structure.

B. Identify the primary cause of caries:
1. Bacterial plaque (Streptococcus mutans).

C. List four contributing factors of caries:
1. Diet
2. Oral hygiene
3. Immune system
4. Personal habits

D. Identify stages of caries development:
1. Demineralization
2. Caries
a. Rampant
b. Recurrent
c. Root caries

E. List four subcomponents of personal habits that are contributing factors of caries:
1. Tobacco
2. Alcohol
3. Sugared soda drinks
4. Gum/candy

F. List five common locations for caries:
1. Pit and fissures
2. Smooth surface
3. Interproximal
4. Root surface/cervical

11.02 Periodontal Disease

A. Define or list the periodontal diseases:
1. Gingivitis
2. Periodontitis

B. Sign and Symptoms:
1. Red, swollen or tender gingival
2. Bleeding gingiva
3. Loose teeth
4. Pain or pressure when chewing
5. Pus

C. Define necrotizing ulcerative periodontitis:

D. Define periodontal pocket:
    1. The disease process causes the normal gingival sulcus to become deeper than normal forming a pocket.

11.03 Attrition, Abrasion, and Erosion

A. Define attrition:
    1. The normal wearing away of tooth structure.

B. Identify the primary cause of accelerated attrition:
    1. Parafunctional habits

C. Identify two parafunctional habits:
    1. Clenching/bruxism
    2. Fibrous foods/chewing tobacco

D. List three contributing factors of attrition:
    1. Abrasive dentifrice
    2. Work environment
    3. Ice chewing

E. Define abrasion:
    1. The abnormal wearing away of tooth structure.

F. List the main cause of abrasion:
    1. Repetitive mechanical habits (i.e., improper toothbrushing).

G. Identify the primary cause of erosion:
    1. Repetitive and prolonged acid contact.

H. List two situations where acid is in prolonged contact with teeth:
    1. Bulimia
    2. Citrus habits

11.04 Soft Tissue Pathology

A. Describe four conditions of the tongue:
    1. Black hairy tongue
    2. Geographic tongue
    3. Fissured tongue
    4. Glossitis

B. Describe five white lesions of the mouth:
    1. Candidiasis (thrush)
    2. Benign hyperkeratosis (leukoplakia or white patches)
    3. Stomatitis nicotina (irritation from smoking)
    4. Chemical burn (aspirin burns)
    5. Trauma

C. Describe three oral lesions of the mouth:
1. Secondary herpetic lesion (cold sore)
2. Aphthous ulcer (canker sore)
3. Mucocele

D. Define seven conditions of the mouth:
1. Torus (exostosis)
2. Irritation fibroma
3. Dry mouth
4. Cyst
5. Papilloma
6. Abscess
7. Cheilitis

E. Define seven abnormalities (developmental) of the mouth:
1. Cleft palate/lip
2. Super numerary
3. Enamel dysplasia
4. Ankyloglossia
5. Macro/Micro dontia
6. Anelogenesis imperfecta
7. Arkylos tooth/impaction

F. Other:
1. Piercings
2. Drug abuse

12.0 EMERGENCY CARE
(I) Number of Tasks to Master = 60
(II) Intended Outcome: Given information about medical and dental emergency care the student will be able to perform 85% of the following tasks on the didactic examination.
(III) Tasks:

12.01 Medical Emergency Care

A. List four vital signs:
1. Temperature
2. Blood pressure
3. Pulse
4. Respiration

B. List four aspects associated with blood pressure:
1. Normal range for blood pressure (90-140/60-90).
2. Recommended technique for obtaining blood pressure.
3. Systolic and diastolic.
4. Health risks associated with high or low blood pressure and its relation to dentistry.

C. List two aspects of heart rate (pulse) and rhythm:
1. Normal range for adult (60-100).
2. Methods for obtaining a reading.

D. List three aspects of respiratory rate:
1. Normal range for adult (12-20).
2. Methods for obtaining a reading.
3. Hyperventilation.

E. List two methods of measuring temperature:
1. Oral
2. Tympanic

F. Describe five ways to prevent emergencies:
1. Obtain current and complete medical/dental history.
2. All dental personnel competent in CPR, Heimlich maneuver, and obtaining vital signs.
3. Assess patient during treatment.
4. Have an office emergency plan.
5. Have emergency equipment ready.

G. Describe the four parts of an emergency preparedness plan:
1. Assigned roles
2. Routine drills
3. Emergency telephone numbers
4. Emergency supplies

H. List four signs of an impending emergency:
1. Change in patient breathing.
2. Change in patent level of consciousness.
3. Change in patient skin color.
4. Change in patient skin temperature.

I. Describe the ABC's of CPR:
1. A = Airway
2. B = Breathing
3. C = Circulation

J. List three signs that indicate it may be necessary to perform the abdominal thrust:
1. The victim clearly indicates they are choking.
2. The victim cannot cough.
3. The victim cannot breathe.

12.02 Medically Compromised Patient

A. Recognize medical conditions that may compromise dental treatment.

B. Identify medications that might affect patient's dental treatment.

C. Recognize the signs and symptoms related to specific medical conditions and emergencies.

12.03 Medical Emergencies

A. Discuss emergency care standards:
1. Allergic.
2. Blood loss.
3. Cardiovascular or cerebrovascular irregularities.
4. Emergencies procedures by metabolic neurologic disease.
5. Respiratory irregularities, obstructions.
6. Shock.
7. Transient unconsciousness.

B. Recognize the signs and symptoms for specific medical emergencies.

C. Explain emergency equipment and supplies.

D. Explain emergency responses.

E. Record documentation of emergency.

12.04 Dental Emergency Care

A. List three steps in responding to an avulsed tooth that will assist in replantation:
1. If tooth is dirty, rinse with tap water. Do not scrub.
2. Gently tease tooth back into socket.
3. Patient to hold in socket while going to dental office.

B. List two steps in responding to an avulsed tooth when replantation is not possible:
1. Place tooth in milk or saline, or place in patient's cheek or a wet towel.
2. Transport to dental office as soon as possible.

C. List three situations when a patient has a fractured tooth and must be treated in a dental office as soon as possible:
1. When there is blood present which appears to be coming from the tooth or immediately around the tooth.
2. When the tooth is subluxed or displaced.
3. When you are unable to calm the patient.

D. List four recommendations for patients experiencing minor dental pain:
1. Take over-the-counter analgesic.
2. Place oil of clove for open cavity.
3. Alternate ice/heat packs 15 minutes on 15 minutes.
4. Rinse with warm salt water for soft tissue.

13.0 DENTAL ANESTHESIA

(I)   Number of Tasks to Master = 75

(II)   Intended Outcome: Given information about dental anesthesia and dental anesthesia terminology, the student will be able to perform 85% of the following tasks with accuracy on the didactic examination.

(III) Tasks:

13.01 Dental Anesthesia Terminology

A. Define the following 16 terms as they apply to dental anesthetic:
1.   Anesthetic: A drug that causes a temporary loss of pain and sensation all or in part.
2.   Analgesic: A drug that relieves pain.
3.   Medical History: A collection of data provided by the patient about his/her general health.
4.   Contraindication: A condition rendering some particular line of treatment not indicated or not advisable.
5.   Epinephrine: A common vasoconstrictor used in local anesthetic, also called adrenaline.
6.   Infiltration Anesthetic: The passage local of anesthetic fluid into tissue spaces to prevent pain.
7.   Block Anesthetic: Local anesthetic injected near a main nerve trunk that prevents any pain sensation from passing from the site to the brain.
8.   Topical Anesthetic: A drug applied topically to oral mucous membrane to numb the area prior to the local anesthetic injection.
9.   Local Anesthetic: A drug injected into tissue to block sensation in a particular area.
10.   Nitrous Oxide: An anesthetic gas used as an analgesic in dentistry; also known as laughing gas.
11.   Dental Syringe: A metal or plastic container with a plunger and needle used for injections of anesthetic into the oral cavity.
12.   Needle Gauge: The diameter of a needle; the needles used in dentistry are usually sizes 27 and 30.
13.   Lumen: The passageway inside a hollow needle or organ.
14.   Diffusion: To spread from an area of high concentration to one of low concentration.
15.   Vasoconstrictor: Drugs that constrict blood vessels around the injection site.
16.   Anaphylaxis: A sudden, severe, and sometimes fatal allergic reaction by an individual to specific allergens.

13.02 Dental Anesthesia

A. List and define the four most commonly used application methods of anesthetics in the dental office:
1.   Topical
2.   Local
3.   Nitrous oxide
4.   Sedation

B. Explain the four important reasons for checking a patient's medical history as it relates to dental anesthetics:
1. A medical history informs the dental staff of a patient's physical condition.
2. Chronic conditions.
3. Allergies.
4. Medications the patient is taking.

C. Explain six health conditions that can affect anesthetic choice:
1. Hypertension
2. Cardiovascular disease
3. Hyperthyroidism
4. Liver disease
5. Kidney disease
6. Pregnancy

D. Identify the seven parts of an aspirating syringe:
1. Thumb-ring
2. Finger grip
3. Finger bar
4. Barrel
5. Piston rod/plunger
6. Harpoon
7. Threaded hub

E. Identify the four parts of a dental anesthetic needle:
1. Plastic housing for needle.
2. Cartridge end of the needle.
3. Needle hub.
4. Injection end of the needle with bevel

F. List the two lengths and gauges of needles most commonly used in dentistry:
1. 1"-30 gauge short (commonly used for infiltration).
2. 1-5/8" – 27 gauge long (commonly used for block).

G. Identify the three parts of an anesthetic cartridge:
1. Rubber stopper
2. Glass cartridge
3. Aluminum cap with rubber diaphragm

H. List the five items needed for giving a local anesthetic injection:
1. Topical anesthetic ointment
2. Sterile cotton tip applicator
3. Sterile gauze sponges (2x2)
4. Needle shield
5. Sterile anesthetic syringe

I. List in order the four steps for topical anesthetic site preparation and delivery:
1. Place a small amount of topical anesthetic on a sterile cotton tip applicator.
2. Dry the proposed site with a sterile 2x2 gauze sponge.

3. Place the topical anesthetic at the prepared site for approximately 2 to 5 minutes.
4. Remove the cotton tip applicator and discard in the designated receptacle.

J. List the seven steps in loading an anesthetic syringe without the needle:
1. Select the type of anesthetic solution as indicated by the dentist and the patient's health history.
2. Hold the syringe in one hand and use the thumb-ring to pull the plunger back for insertion of the anesthetic cartridge.
3. With the other hand, load the anesthetic cartridge into the syringe barrel opening; the stopper end goes first toward the plunger.
4. Release the thumb-ring and allow the harpoon to engage into the rubber stopper.
5. Use the other hand to apply firm pressure or gentle tapping to engage the plunger harpoon into the stopper.
6. Check to make sure the harpoon is securely engaged with the rubber stopper.
7. Gently pull back on the plunger to make sure the dentist can aspirate the anesthetic during the injection.

K. List the six steps for attaching the needle to the anesthetic syringe:
1. Break the seal on the needle and remove the protective cap from the insertion area of the needle.
2. Carefully align and screw the end of the needle into position on the syringe.
3. Position the needle so it is straight and firmly attached to the diaphragm part of the cartridge, already in the syringe.
4. Dispel a very small amount of anesthetic to confirm engagement.
5. Gently pull back on the plunger to make sure aspiration is confirmed.
6. Place the prepared syringe on the tray ready for use and out of sight of the patient.

L. List the five steps for safely passing the anesthetic syringe to the dentist:
1. Loosen the needle guard.
2. Check the needle guard for stability.
3. Place the thumb-ring over the dentist's thumb, and at the same time, rotate the syringe barrel so the glass cartridge is in full view.
4. Gently but carefully and smoothly remove the needle guard as the dentist takes the syringe.
5. Put the needle guard in the needle holder. The dentist will put the used syringe into the holder, needle first, for protection of the staff.

M. List the two necessary steps needed for recapping and discarding the anesthetic needle:
1. The dental assistant or hygienist or dentist may recap the needle only by use of a needle guard or a one-handed scoop. (This procedure is usually completed by the dentist for employee protection as required by OSHA regulations.)
2. The used anesthetic needle must be discarded in a sharps container.

14.0 CHAIRSIDE ASSISTING

(I)   Number of Tasks to Master = 66

(II) ˈIntended Outcome: Given information about dental ergonomics, principles of four-handed dentistry and maintaining a clear operating field, the student will perform 85% of the following tasks with accuracy on the didactic examination.

(I)   Tasks:

14.01 Dental Ergonomics

A. Define the five classifications of motion:
   1. Class I: Movement of the fingers only, as when picking up a cotton roll.
   2. Class II: Fingers and wrist motion, as used when transferring an instrument to the operator.
   3. Class III: Fingers, wrist, and elbow motion, as when reaching for a handpiece.
   4. Class IV: Movement of the entire arm and shoulder, as when reaching into a supply tub or container.
   5. Class V: Movement of the entire torso, as when turning around to reach for equipment from a side or split delivery unit.

B. List the four zones of activity:
   1. Operator's zone
   2. Assistant's zone
   3. Transfer zone
   4. Static zone

C. Describe the activities of the above four zones:
   1. Operator's Zone: Where the operator is positioned to access the oral cavity and have the best visibility.
   2. Assistant's Zone: Where the assistant is positioned to easily assist the dentist and have access to instruments, the evacuator, and so on, on the dental cart or cart without interference.
   3. Transfer Zone: Where instruments and materials are passed and received.
   4. Static Zone: Where rear delivery systems, dental instruments, mobile cart, and equipment can be found.

D. Using the face of a clock, define each zone of activity for the right-handed dentist:
   1. Operator: 7 o'clock to 12 o'clock
   2. Static: 12 o'clock to 2 o'clock
   3. Assistant: 2 o'clock to 4 o'clock
   4. Transfer: 4 o'clock to 7 o'clock

E. Using the face of a clock, define each zone of activity for the left-handed dentist:
   1. Operator: 12 o'clock to 5 o'clock
   2. Transfer: 5 o'clock to 8 o'clock
   3. Assistant: 8 o'clock to 10 o'clock
   4. Static: 10 o'clock to 12 o'clock

F. Define the three commonly used patient positions in general dentistry:
  1. Upright Position: The back of the chair is upright at a 90° angle. This position is used for patient entry and dismissal, and while taking radiographs or impressions.
  2. Supine Position: The back of the chair is lowered back until the patient's head and knees are at the same plane. Most dental treatment takes place in the supine position.
  3. Subsupine Position: The back of the chair is lowered until the patient's head is lower than the feet. This position is only recommended in emergency situations.

G. List four criteria for positioning the operator:
  1. Back straight, feet on the floor, and thighs angled so that the knees are slightly lower than hip level.
  2. Elbows close to the sides with shoulders relaxed.
  3. Patient's oral cavity should be at elbow height.
  4. The operator should be facing forward with eyes focused downward.

H. List four criteria for positioning the dental assistant:
  1. Back straight with eye level approximately four to six inches higher than the operator.
  2. Torso centered on the stool, with the stool as close to the patient as possible.
  3. Feet positioned on the ring or platform near the base of the stool.
  4. The assistant's body is facing toward the patient's head, with hips and thighs level to the floor and parallel to the patient's shoulders.

14.02 Principles of Four-Handed Dentistry

A. Define four-handed or sit-down dentistry:
  1. The dentist and dental assistant are working together at the dental chair in an effort to provide a smooth and efficient transfer of instruments and materials during patient procedures.

B. List three benefits of four-handed dentistry:
  1. Increased patient comfort and safety.
  2. Decreased stress and fatigue for the operator and assistant.
  3. Increased production with decreased chair time.

C. List six general rules of transferring instruments:
  1. Pass with the left hand (right-handed operator).
  2. Never pass instruments over the patient's face.
  3. Avoid moving the operator's hand and eyes from the working site.
  4. Always wait for a signal from the operator before exchanging instruments.
  5. Keep the passing zone close to the face, a few inches below the chin.
  6. Pass the instrument in the position of use.

D. Define the three types of instrument grasps:
  1. Pen Grasp: The instrument is held in the same manner as a pen.
  2. Palm Grasp: The instrument is held in the palm of the hand.

3. Palm-Thumb Grasp: The instrument is held in the palm of the hand and the thumb is used to stabilize the instrument.

E. Define the two most commonly used types of instrument transfers:
    1. One-handed Transfer: The assistant passes and receives the instrument with one hand allowing for the use of the evacuator or the air-water syringe at the same time.
    2. Two-handed Transfer: The assistant uses both hands for the transfer, one to ass and the other to receive.

14.03 Maintaining a Clear Operating Field

A. List six responsibilities the dental assistant has in maintaining a clear operating field:
    1. Adjust the dental light so the light shines directly on the area where the operator is working.
    2. Use retraction techniques to keep tissues out of the operator's way.
    3. Use evacuator to remove water, saliva, and debris from the patient's mouth.
    4. Keep the operator's mirror clear during treatment.
    5. Rinse and dry the area where the operator is working.
    6. Help keep the patient's mouth open during the treatment.

B. List two evacuation methods:
    1. Saliva ejector
    2. High-volume evacuator (HVE)

C. List three isolation techniques:
    1. Cotton rolls
    2. Dry-angles and other related aids
    3. Dental (rubber) dam

D. List two grasps that an oral evacuator may be held in:
    1. Palm-thumb grasp
    2. Pen grasp

E. List six guidelines for oral evacuation tip placement:
    1. Hold in right hand for right-handed operator.
    2. Carefully place the evacuator tip in the patient's mouth; avoid bumping the teeth, lips, or gingiva.
    3. Place the evacuator tip approximately one tooth distal to the tooth being worked on.
    4. Hold the bevel of the evacuator tip parallel to the buccal or lingual surface of the tooth.
    5. The middle of the evacuator tip opening should be even with the occlusal surface and held still so that it does not draw the water coolant away from the bur.
    6. Keep the evacuator tip far enough away from the mucosal tissue to prevent it from being sucked into the tip.

15.0 DENTAL MATERIALS

(I)   Number of Tasks to Master = 82
(II) Intended Outcome: Given information about the properties and different classifications of dental materials, the student will be able to perform 85% of the following tasks with accuracy on the didactic examination.
(III) Tasks:

15.01 Properties and Classifications of Dental Materials

A. List the four properties a dental material must display to be used successfully to restore oral structures:
   1. Durability
   2. Corrosion resistance
   3. Non-toxicity
   4. Bio-compatibility

B. List and define the three properties of dental materials listed below which are evaluated to determine the materials suitability for use in the mouth:
   1. Stress: The force (per unit body) within a body that resists an external force.
   2. Strain: The distortion within a body that results from an applied force.
   3. Strength: The maximum stress required to fracture a structure.

C. Define restorative dentistry.

D. List six classifications of dental materials:
   1. Metals
   2. Resins
   3. Impression materials
   4. Gypsums
   5. Cements and liners
   6. Porcelain and ceramics

15.02 Metals in Dentistry

A. List four uses of metals in dentistry:
   1. Crowns and bridge restorations
   2. Partial dentures
   3. Implants
   4. Amalgam restorations

B. Explain six important information points about amalgam:
   1. Amalgam is the most common and widely used dental restorative worldwide.
   2. The American Dental Association and various independent agencies have studied the mercury in amalgam and reported no adverse effects.
   3. Mercury is needed to make the material into a paste form, which allows it to be placed into the tooth preparation.
   4. The mercury is lost during condensation into the tooth and over the life of the restoration as mercury vapor. (Use no touch technique.)

5. Amalgam breaks down by corrosion over time requiring replacement.
6. Amalgam is an unusual alloy composed of silver, tin, copper, and mercury.

15.03 Resins in Dentistry

A. Explain how to prepare, mix, deliver, and store dental resins:
   1. Acrylic Resins: Primarily used for denture bases and provisional (temporary) crown and bridge restoration.
   2. Composite Resins: Primarily used for restorations and cements.
   3. Glass Ionomers: Used as cements, liners, bases, and restorations.
   4. Compomers: A combination of glass ionomer and composite that is used primarily as a restorative, particularly for pediatric dentistry, because it inherently releases fluoride to the tooth structure once it is placed.

B. List the two types of bonds that occur in the resin-to-tooth bond:
   1. Mechanical
   2. Chemical

C. Explain why phosphoric acid is used to etch the surface of the enamel and dentin.
   1. This creates micro-crevasses that the liquid of the bonding agent enters into. When the bonding agent is set, it becomes a tiny finger that grabs onto microporosities and fissures in the tooth surface.

D. Explain when the chemical bond occurs:
   1. When the etchant breaks down the enamel land dentin exposing the organic component of the structure. These are primarily collagen fibers. The bonding agent has a chemical affinity to collagen, so it attaches to it.

15.04 Impression Materials in Dentistry

A. Explain how to prepare, mix, and deliver three major types of impression materials:
   1. Wax
   2. Hydrocolloid
   3. Elastomer

B. Explain the purpose of was as an impression material:
   1. To take bite registrations.

C. List two forms of hydrocolloid impression material and state their use:
   1. Reversible: Crown and bridge impressions.
   2. Irreversible (alginate): Study model impressions.

D. List the four forms of elastomeric impression materials:
   1. Polysulfide
   2. Polyether
   3. Addition reaction silicone (polyvinyl siloxane or vinyl polysiloxane)
   4. Condensation reaction silicone

E. Explain what "addition reaction silicone" is:
1. Used in a putty wash technique.
2. The most commonly used elastomeric impression material.

15.05 Gypsums Materials in Dentistry

A. Regarding gypsum-based materials (plaster), explain what will happen if the water-to-powder ratio varies from optimum:
1. The plaster will weaken.

B. Explain how to prepare, mix, deliver, and store gypsum products (plasters) according to ADA Spec #, Traditional Name, and Traditional Color.

ADA Spec #	Traditional Name	Traditional Color
Type I	Impression Plaster	Variable
Type II	Lab. or Model Plaster	White
Type III	Class I Dental Stone	Yellow
Type IV	Class II Dental Stone or Improved Stone	Green, Blue, or Pink

15.06 Cements and Liners in Dentistry

A. Describe three liners:
1. Calcium hydroxide
2. Cavity varnish
3. Fluoride varnish/sealants

B. Describe three uses of cements:
1. Luting
2. Temporary fillings
3. Base fillings

C. Explain how to prepare, mix, deliver, and store dental cements:
1. Glass ionomer
2. Zinc phosphate
3. Polycarboxylate
4. Zinc oxide eugenol
5. Composite resin

D. List five considerations when mixing cements:
1. Read and follow manufacturer directions.
2. Measure carefully.
3. Avoid moisture contamination.
4. Mix powder into liquid
5. Allow to set completely or according to directions.

15.07 Porcelain and Ceramics in Dentistry

A. List the five major uses of porcelain in the dental office:
1. Porcelain is used as a coating of porcelain fused to metal crowns.
2. Porcelain is used as a crown material that can be bonded directly to the tooth.
3. Porcelain is used as an inlay/onlay material that can be bonded directly into the tooth.
4. Porcelain is used as teeth in dentures.
5. Porcelain is often used as a veneering material that can be bonded to tooth structure directly.

15.08 Other Dental Materials

A. Explain how to prepare, mix, deliver, and store the following:
1. Sedative dressings
2. Peridontal surgical dressings
3. Post surgical dressings
4. Bleaching agents
5. Bonding agents
6. Endodontic materials
7. Etchants
8. Pit and fissure sealants

15.09 Lab Procedures

A. Describe the following laboratory procedures:
1. Fabricate diagnostic casts.
2. Trimming diagnostic cast.
3. Debride and polish fixed and removable appliances and prosthesis.
4. Splints.
5. Fabricate custom impression trays, mouth/athletic guards, bleaching trays, acrylic temps, etc.

16.0 INTRODUCTION TO DENTAL RADIOGRAPHY

(I) Number of Tasks to Master = 190
(II) Intended Outcome: Given information about biological effects of ionizing radiation, health protection techniques, x-ray machines, dental film/sensors, radiographic landmarks, mounting radiographs and processing procedures, the student will be able to perform 85% of the following tasks with accuracy on the didactic examination.
(III) Tasks:

16.01 Biological Effects of Ionizing Radiation

A. List four tissues/cells that are highly sensitive to radiation:
1. Bone marrow
2. Reproductive cells
3. Intestines
4. Lymphoid tissue

B. List ten tissues/cells that are moderately sensitive to radiation:
1. Oral mucosa
2. Skin
3. Growing bone
4. Growing cartilage
5. Small vasculature
6. Connective tissue
7. Salivary glands
8. Mature bone
9. Mature cartilage
10. Thyroid gland tissue

C. List six tissues/cells that have low sensitivity to radiation:
1. Liver
2. Optic lens
3. Kidneys
4. Muscle
5. Nerve
6. Brain

16.02 Health Protection Techniques

A. List three methods of operator protection from primary radiation:
1. Stand behind a protective barrier.
2. Avoid standing in the path of the direct beam of radiation.
3. Never hold the film for the patient during an exposure.

B. List three methods of operator protection from radiation leakage from suspected x-ray machine malfunction:
1. Do not hold the tube housing or the Position Indicating Device (PID) during an exposure.
2. Have the machine tested every two years.
3. Wear a monitoring device or use area monitors to test for unwanted exposure.

C. List three methods of operator protection from secondary/scattered radiation:
1. Stand behind the patient at a point between 90° and 135° from the source of the beam.
2. Stand behind a wall or radiation-resistant barrier, or at least six feet away from the radiation source.
3. Use of radiation monitoring devices—film badges or dosimeters.

D. List the six methods of radiation protection for the patient:
1. Use the fastest film speed available—E-speed.
2. Use open-ended, shielded, Position Indicating Devices no larger than 2.75 inches in diameter—rectangular devices are superior.
3. Use good technique to diminish the need for retaking films.
4. Carefully follow manufacturer's directions for processing.
5. Use lead aprons and thyroid collars to cover the patient.
6. ALARA (as low as reasonably achievable).

16.03 The X-ray Machine

A. List the five major components of the x-ray machine:
1. Tube
2. Glass housing
3. Tubehead
4. Position Indicating Device (cone)
    a. Collimation
    b. Filtration
5. Control panel adjustments

B. Describe the five major components of the x-ray machine:
1. Tube: Contains negative (cathode) and the positive (anode) terminals that first create, then attract electrons to produce x-rays.
2. Glass Housing: Leaded glass that surrounds the tube.
3. Tubehead: Heavy metal enclosure that surrounds the x-ray tube.
4. Position Indicating Device (cone): Used to direct and contain the beam of radiation.
5. Control panel adjustments.

16.04 Dental Film/Sensors

A. List four types of dental films:
1. Intraoral
    a. Film sizes
2. Extraoral
    a. Film sizes
3. Duplicating
4. Digital
    a. Charge-coupled device (CCD)
    b. Complementary metal oxidesemiconductor/active pixel sensor (CMOS/APS)
    c. Charge injection device (CID)

B. Describe film selection and uses:
1. Perical
2. Bitewing
3. Occlusal
4. Panoramic
5. Other extraoral

C. List three factors to consider when storing dental film:
1. Temperature
2. Humidity
3. Radiation

D. Explain the three important film storage factors:
1. Optimum temperature for storage should be between 50° and 70° Fahrenheit.
2. The relative humidity for film storage should be between 30% and 50%.

3. Film should be stored in areas where radiation exposures are made.

E. List three factors to consider relevant to inventory control of dental film:
   1. Shelf-life
   2. Numbering system
   3. Packaging

F. Explain the three inventory control factors:
   1. Examine the manufacturer's expiration date on film boxes and store so the oldest film is used first.
   2. Store film according to size—number 0 smallest, to number 4, largest (0, 1, 2 most common).
   3. Store film by package type—single film packets or double film packets.

G. Explain film composition:
   1. Latent image
   2. Film base
   3. Adhesive layer
   4. Gelatin

16.05 Radiographic Techniques

A. Paralleling Technique:
   1. Advantages and disadvantages
   2. Accessories used
   3. Film size and type required

B. Bisecting angle technique:
   1. Advantages and disadvantages
   2. Accessories used
   3. Film size and type required

C. Extra oral film:
   1. Advantages and disadvantages
   2. Accessories used
   3. Film size and type required

16.06 Radiographic Infection Control

A. Define two image characteristics used to identify landmarks visible in radiographic films.
   1. Radiopaque
   2. Radiolucent

16.07 Patient Management for Radiography

A. Use appropriate patient management techniques before, during, and after exposure:
   1. Patient concerns
   2. Special needs patients

16.08 Radiographic Landmarks

A. Define five image characteristics used to identify landmarks visible in radiographic films:
1. Radiopaque
2. Radiolucent
3. Density
4. Contrast
5. Sharpness

B. Identify six landmarks visible in the maxillary molar film:
1. Maxillary sinus
2. Zygomatic process
3. Zygomatic bone
4. Hamulus
5. Maxillary tuberosity
6. Coronoid process of the mandible

C. Identify one landmark visible in the maxillary premolar film:
1. Maxillary sinus

D. Identify two landmarks visible in the maxillary canine film:
1. Maxillary sinus
2. Junction of the maxillary sinus and nasal fossa

E. Identify five landmarks visible in the maxillary incisor film:
1. Incisive foramen
2. Nasal septum
3. Nasal fossa
4. Anterior nasal spine
5. Median palatine suture

F. Identify four landmarks visible in the mandibular molar film:
1. Mandibular canal
2. Internal oblique line
3. External oblique ridge
4. Mylohyoid ridge

G. Identify one landmark visible in the mandibular premolar film:
1. Mental foramen

H. Identify three landmarks visible in the mandibular incisor film:
1. Lingual foramen
2. Mental ridge
3. Genial tubercles

16.09 Mounting Radiographs

A. Describe the eight-step procedure for mounting a full mouth set of radiographs:
1. Mark the mount with the patient name, age, date.
2. Place a clean, dry paper towel on the countertop in front of a lighted viewbox.
3. With clean, dry hands, handle radiographs by edges only.
4. Place all radiographs on the paper towel with the embossed (raised) dot facing up.
5. Sort the radiographs into three groups: bitewings, posterior periapicals, and anterior periapicals.
6. Further arrange the radiographs by maxillary arch: Posterior and anterior, and mandibular arch: posterior and anterior.
7. Separate all films left from right and orient periapical films with maxillary roots pointing up and mandibular roots pointing down.
8. Begin mounting by inserting the bitewing radiographs into the mount, followed by the posterior periapicals and finally the anterior periapicals.

16.10 Processing Procedures

A. Describe the six steps required during film processing to assure proper infection control:
1. Wipe saliva from films.
2. Place films in a labeled disposable container.
3. Wash hands.
4. With non-powdered gloved hands, and in safelight conditions, open the film packets by pulling on their tabs.
5. Allow films to drop onto a clean paper towel or into a paper cup.
6. Remove contaminated gloves, rewash hands, and re-glove prior to processing. NOTE: An alternative is to wear over gloves when opening film packets.

B. State the ten steps required to hand process films:
1. Check solution levels.
2. Maintain appropriate chemical temperatures: between 68° and 70°.
3. Turn white lights off and safelight on.
4. Using appropriate methods of infection control, remove films from packets.
5. Securely place films onto hanger.
6. Immerse film in developer and activate timer for five minutes.
7. Remove from developer and rinse by agitation for 30 seconds.
8. Immerse films in fixer and activate timer for 10 minutes.
9. Remove films and place in circulating water bath for 10 minutes.
10. Dry films in electric dryer or air-dry until films are no longer tacky.

C. State four principles of operation for automatic processing:
1. Manufacturer's recommendations must be followed precisely.
2. Rollers or tracks are used to transport the films through the processing chemicals.
3. Much higher temperatures are required for automatic processing.

4. Chemical concentrations are higher for automatic processing.

D. Describe three elements of caring for the automatic processor:
  1. Special cleaning films must be run through the system daily.
  2. Depending on usage, the processor must be scoured with a nylon pad weekly or biweekly. Harsh cleansers should not be used.
  3. At the same time interval, the rollers should be removed from roller-type systems and soaked in warm water for 20 minutes, then special cleaning solutions used.

E. Describe the three principles for care of processing solutions:
  1. Levels of the solutions must be checked regularly and replenished as required by manufacturer recommendation.
  2. If large films such as panoramic films are processed frequently, the solutions will need to be replenished more often.
  3. Solutions should be changed at least every four weeks.

F. Describe quality assurance procedures:
  1. Recording solution temperatures.
  2. Dates of solution changes.
  3. Test films.
  4. Equipment maintenance
  5. Inspections

16.11 Evaluating Radiographs for Diagnostic Value

A. Identify interoral exposure errors and causes.
  1. Elongation
  2. Foreshortening
  3. Horizontal overlap
  4. Cone cutting
  5. Light image
  6. Dark image
  7. Film bending
  8. Reverse film (herringbone effect)
  9. Black (clear) film
  10. Blurred image
  11. Superimposed image
  12. Double exposure
  13. Saliva lead
  14. Film placement errors

B. Identify extraoral exposure errors and cause:
  1. Patient positioning errors
  2. Film placement errors

C. Identify processing errors and causes:
  1. Spots on film
  2. Fogging
  3. Light and dark images
  4. Clear (blank) film

5. Particle images
6. Stains
7. Discoloration
8. Overlapped films
9. Air bubbles
10. Scratches
11. White or black lines
12. Static electricity artifacts
13. Fingerprints

SECTION 2: CLINICAL EDUCATION: FUNDAMENTALS OF DENTAL ASSISTING

Unit	Title	Number of Tasks

Table 2. Educational Parameters of the Clinical/Lab Component of the Fundamentals of Dental Assisting Curriculum: Procedures

Unit	Title	Number of Tasks
1	Disclosing Procedure	5
2	Brushing Procedure	12
3	Flossing Procedure	7
4	Vital Signs Measurement Procedure	7
5	Personal Protective Equipment (PPE) Procedure	11
6	Mounting Radiographs Procedure	6
7	Acrylic Disk Polishing Procedure	7
8	Diagnostic Cast Procedure (Working with Alginate and Dental Plaster Lab)	20
9	Treatment Room Breakdown Procedure	17
	Total	92

1.0 DISCLOSING PROCEDURE

(I) Number of Tasks to Master = 5

(II) Intended Outcome: Given disclosing tablets or disclosing solution, lip lubricant, safety glasses, gloves, mask, soap, paper towels, mouth mirror, hand mirror, cotton tip applicator, cup, water, and a sink (if available), the student will perform the following tasks on a partner with 100% accuracy.

(III) Tasks:

1. Take universal precautions.

2. Apply lip lubricant on partner's lips.

3. Refer to manufacturer's instructions prior to using the disclosing solution or tablets. If using disclosing tablets, have your partner chew one table thoroughly, swish with water, and expectorate (spit) into a cup or sink. If using the disclosing solution, apply a small amount of solution on a cotton tip applicator and glide the applicator over all the surfaces of the teeth. Instruct your partner to rinse with water and expectorate into a cup or sink.

4. Using a mouth mirror, look in your partner's mouth and identify the areas of plaque on the surfaces of the teeth. Holding a hand mirror, your partner will also look in the mouth and identify the areas of plaque on tooth surfaces. (NOTE: Areas where plaque is present on the teeth will stain a color.)

5. Disinfect the surface area where you are working. Your partner will follow the same procedures (1-4).

2.0 BRUSHING PROCEDURE

(I) Number of Tasks to Master = 12

III) Intended Outcome: Given a mouth mirror and soft bristle toothbrush, the student will perform the following tasks with 100% accuracy.

(III) Tasks:

1. Grasp the toothbrush with a firm grip and utilize a hand mirror to assess tooth brushing technique.

2. Begin on the maxillary buccal surfaces of the two most posterior teeth. Angle the toothbrush at a 45° angle to the long axis of the tooth.

3. Choosing no more than two teeth at a time, gently move the toothbrush against the teeth and gums using small vibratory strokes. Brush for a count of 10.

4. Continue around the mouth until all the buccal and facial surfaces have been brushed.

5. Begin on the maxillary lingual surfaces of the two most posterior teeth and continue until all the lingual surfaces have been brushed.

6. Begin on the mandibular quadrant on the buccal surfaces of the two most posterior teeth. Angle the toothbrush at a 45° angle to the long axis of the tooth.

7. Choosing no more than two teeth at a time, gently move the toothbrush against the teeth and gums using small vibratory strokes. Brush for a count of 10.

8. Continue around the mouth until all the buccal and facial tooth surfaces have been brushed.

9. Continue on the mandibular lingual surfaces of the two most posterior teeth and continue until all the lingual surfaces have been brushed.

10. Begin on the furthermost tooth in a maxillary quadrant. Place the bristles on the chewing surface of the teeth and use a back-and-forth motion across the occlusal surfaces. Brush from the furthermost tooth toward the premolars for a count of 10.

11. Continue until all the occlusal surfaces have been brushed.

12. Rinse to remove plaque and debris

3.0   FLOSSING PROCEDURE
(I)   Number of Tasks to Master = 7
(II)   Intended Outcome: Using waxed or unwaxed dental floss, a hand mirror, and the assistance of a partner, the student will perform the following tasks on themselves with 100% accuracy.
(III) Tasks:

1. Your partner will hold the hand mirror while you practice. Remove a piece of floss approximately 18 inches long.

2. Wrap the ends of the floss around your middle fingers until the length of the floss is approximately two inches. Use your other fingers to help guide the floss.

3. Beginning on the most posterior interproximal surface of a mandibular or maxillary tooth, glide the floss between the teeth using a back-and-forth motion. Avoid snapping the floss against the gum tissue.

4. Curve the floss in a C-shape around the tooth. Guide the floss into the sulcus maintaining a C-shape. Gently floss the area four to five times using an up and down motion.

5. Remove the floss from the sulcus area and curve the floss in a C-shape around the opposing tooth. Glide the floss into the sulcus, maintaining a C-shape. Gently floss the area four to five times using an up and down motion.

6. Remove the floss from the contact area with an upward gliding motion. Unwrap the floss from the fingers and wrap a new section of unused floss around the same fingers. Proceed to the next interproximal area.

7. Continue in this manner until all the interproximal surfaces have been flossed.

4.0 VITAL SIGNS PROCEDURE
(I) Number of Tasks to Master = 7
(II) Intended Outcome: Given the knowledge of vital statistics, a sphygmomanometer, a stethoscope, a thermometer, a timepiece, a chart, a writing instrument, and a patient, the student will perform the following tasks with 100% accuracy.
(III) Tasks:

1. Have the patient bare an arm without obstruction up to the shoulder.

2. Place the sphygmomanometer around the upper arm between the shoulder and the elbow, with the pressure gauge tubing lined up over the medial aspect of the antecubital fossa.

3. Place the earpieces of the stethoscope in the ears and the tympanic piece over the brachial artery in the antecubital fossa.

4. Inflate the cuff until there is not a pulse sound appreciated through the stethoscope (usually 160 to 180).

5. As pressure is released from the cuff, record the pressure reading on the gauge when you first hear a pulse sound then again when the pulse sound is no longer heard.

6. Place the pads of the index and middle fingers on the inner surface of the patient's wrist (between the radius and the tendon). Start counting with 0 for the first pulse; the next pulse will be counted as 1 and so on. Count the pulse for thirty seconds and then multiply by 2 to complete the rate for one full minute.

7. Using a timepiece and watching the patient, count the number of breaths taken in a 20 second period, multiply this number by three, and then record the number.

5.0 PERSONAL PROTECTIVE EQUIPMENT PROCEDURE
(I) Number of Tasks to Master = 11
(II) Intended Outcome: Given the necessary personnel supplies (lab jacket, gloves, masks, and goggles) to don and take off personal protective equipment, the student will perform the following tasks with 100% accuracy.
(III) Tasks:

5.01 Don Personal Protective Equipment

1. Put on fresh lab jacket and fasten properly.

2. Put on protective eyewear.

3. Place mask on face and fasten properly; adjust the nose area to fit snugly.

4. Wash and dry hands, then put on exam gloves.

5. Tuck cuff of sleeves into the gloves.

5.02 Removing Personal Protective Equipment

1. Grasp the cuff of the first glove and pull it off, turning it inside out. As you do, keep this glove in the gloved hand.

2. With the ungloved hand, grasp the inside of the cuff of the other glove, pull the glove off turning it inside out, keeping the first glove inside. Throw the gloves in the proper waste receptacle.

3. Grasp the elastic or ties of the mask and remove it from the face, being cautious not to touch the contaminated front area. Throw the mask away.

4. Grasp the protective eyewear by the earpiece and remove from the face. Place by sink to clean and disinfect.

5. Remove the lab jacket and place in the proper area.

6. Wash hands.

6.0 MOUNTING RADIOGRAPHS PROCEDURE
(I) Number of Tasks to Master = 6
(II) Intended Outcome: Given the knowledge of dental anatomy, eighteen (18) developed radiographs, a mount, table surface, and a light source, the student will be able to perform the following tasks with 100% accuracy.
(III) Tasks:

1. Arrange all dental films with dimples facing up from table top.

2. Group bitewings, anterior periapicals, and posterior periapicals.

3. Separate maxillary from mandibular periapicals.

4. Separate all films left and right. (NOTE: With the dimple facing toward the reader, identify the teeth in the radiograph and place with teeth anteriorly to center of the mount.

5. Insert each film into the appropriate slot on the x-ray mount (dimple facing up).

6.   Label the mounts with patient name and date.

7.0   ACRYLIC DISK POLISHING PROCEDURE
(I)   Number of Tasks to Master = 7

(II)   Intended Outcome: Given the necessary didactic instruction, supplies, and equipment to perform polishing acrylic, the student will perform the following tasks on an acrylic disk with imperfections with 100% accuracy.

(III)   Tasks:

1.   Assemble acrylic disk polishing tray set up.
   a.   Gloves
   b.   Eyewear
   c.   Acrylic disc
   d.   Lathe
   e.   Arbor band or latch-type acrylic bur
   f.   Slow speed handpiece
   g.   Wet-rag wheel
   h.   Medium grit pumice
   i.   Flour of pumice

2.   Take required safety precautions.

3.   Reduce the bulk with the arbor band on the lathe or an acrylic bur in the handpiece.

4.   Refine surface with an acrylic bur in the handpiece.

5.   Polish on low with a wet-rag wheel and medium pumice.

6.   Polish on low with a wet-rag wheel and flour of pumice.

7.   Rinse and evaluate disk.

8.0   DIAGNOSTIC CAST PROCEDURE (WORKING WITH ALGINATE AND DENTAL PLASTER LABORATORY)
(I)   Number of Tasks to Master = 20

(II)   Intended Outcome: Given the necessary diagnostic casting equipment and supplies, the student will perform the following tasks with 100% accuracy.

(III)   Tasks:

1.   Assemble the diagnostic cast procedure tray set up.
   a.   Flexible mixing bowl
   b.   Large mixing spatula
   c.   Small mixing spatula
   d.   Vibrator
   e.   Dental model plaster
   f.   Rubber model base formers
   g.   Maxillary stock tray to fit the typodont model
   h.   Mandibular stock tray to fit the typodont model
   i.   Typodont model

j. Sink for water and hand washing

k. Paper towels

l. Gloves

2. Produce a diagnostic model of the dental arches by performing the following twenty tasks:

   a. Wash, dry, and glove hands.

   b. Select a tray that will fit the typodont model provided.

   c. Measure out the alginate powder.

   d. Measure out the correct amount of water.

   e. Pour the alginate into the mixing bowl.

   f. Pour the water into the mixing bowl.

   g. Mix the material until the mix is creamy, remembering to keep the amount of air incorporation to a minimum to prevent bubble formation.

   h. Load the mandibular tray.

   i. Place the loaded tray onto the mandibular teeth of the typodont in a manner that simulates insertion into an actual patient's mouth. This must be done remembering to seat the posterior section of the tray first and then rocking it onto the anterior teeth.

   j. Once the material is set, remove the impression from the typodont and repeat the procedures for the upper arch.

   k. Have the instructor check the impressions to ensure all the teeth are registered without excessive show-through on the occlusal, that the extensions of the impressions are appropriate (i.e., vestibules, palate, throat) and that all the teeth are properly registered.

   l. Proceed to pour-up the impressions by measuring the dental plaster into the flexible bowl.

   m. Measure out the correct amount of water and pour it into the mixing bowl.

   n. Mix the material with the intention of preventing a lot of air incorporation, check consistency (smooth and creamy with body) and use the vibrator to eliminate as much of the incorporated air as possible from the mix.

   o. Pour the impressions by dipping a small amount of plaster out of the mix with a mixing spatula and running the mixture into the impression from one point using the vibrator to help the material slowly advance to each of the teeth and other features of the impression.

   p. Lay the poured impression aside for a moment while a sufficient quantity of the mixed plaster is loaded into the rubber base former.

   q. Invert the poured impression over the base former and seat without embedding the tray itself in the plaster.

   r. Repeat these procedures with the other impression.

   s. Once the plaster is set (45-60 minutes), remove the impressions from the new model without breaking teeth.

   t. Have the instructor inspect the study model to determine acceptability.

9.0 TREATMENT ROOM BREAKDOWN PROCEDURE

(I) Number of Tasks to Master = 17

(II) Intended Outcome: Given the necessary didactic instruction, supplies and equipment to breakdown a dental treatment room, the student will perform the following tasks with 100% accuracy.

(III) Tasks:

1. Remove mask and gloves following completion of the dental procedure. Leave safety glasses on.

2. Complete chart entry.

3. Walk patient out to the front desk.

4. Return to treatment room.

5. Put on utility gloves.

6. Clear tray of disposables.

7. Place items into the biobag at the unit.

8. Run handpieces 30 seconds.

9. Remove handpieces and place on tray.

10. Strip barriers off of chair, stools, cart, and light.

11. Wipe handpieces, HVE, a/w syringes with disinfectant.

12. Lay handpieces, HVE, a/w syringes on a paper towel and spray them with an acceptable disinfectant.

13. Take tray of contaminated items to the sterilization area and separate.

14. Remove the barrier from the instrument tray.

15. Return to the treatment room, spray glasses with disinfectant.

16. Spray utility gloves with disinfectant.

17. Wash hands.

Table 3. Educational Parameters of the Clinical/Lab Component of the Fundamentals of Dental Assisting Curriculum: Evaluation

Unit	Title	Number of Tasks
1	Disclosing Procedure	5
2	Brushing Procedure	12
3	Flossing Procedure	7
4	Vital Signs Procedure	7
5	Personal Protective Equipment Procedure	11
6	Mounting Radiographs Procedure	6
7	Acrylic Disk Polishing Procedure	7
8	Diagnostic Cast Procedure	20
9	Treatment Room Breakdown Procedure	17
	Total	92

FUNDAMENTALS OF DENTAL ASSISTING
COMPETENCY-BASED CLINICAL EVALUATION

1.0   DISCLOSING PROCEDURE

Student Name:_____

Lab Evaluator:_____Date_____ Grade: [ ] Pass [ ] Fail

CL Evaluator:_____Date_____ Grade: [ ] Pass [ ] Fail

Intended Outcome: Given disclosing tablets or disclosing solution, lip lubricant, safety glasses, gloves, mask, soap, paper towels, mouth mirror, hand mirror, cotton tip applicator, cup, water, and a sink (if available), the student will perform the following tasks on themselves and their partner with 100% accuracy.

	Tasks	Clinical/Laboratory	
		Pass	Fail
1.	Take universal precautions		
2.	Apply lip lubricant on partner's lips.		
3.	Refer to manufacturer's instruction prior to using the disclosing solution or tablets. If using tablets, have your partner chew one tablet thoroughly, swish with water and expectorate (spit) into a cup or sink. If using the disclosing solution, apply a small amount of solution on a cotton tip applicator and glide the applicator over all the surfaces of the teeth. Instruct your partner to rinse with water and expectorate into a cup or sink.		
4.	Using a mouth mirror, look in your partner's mouth and identify the areas of plaque on the surface of the teeth. Holding a hand mirror, your partner will also look in the mouth and identify areas of plaque on tooth surfaces. (Note: Areas where plaque is present on the teeth will stain a color.)		
5.	Disinfect the surface area where you are working. Your partner will follow the same procedure (Steps 1-4 above).		
Comments			

2.0 BRUSHING PROCEDURE

Student Name:_____

Lab Evaluator:_____Date_____ Grade: [ ] Pass [ ] Fail

CL Evaluator:_____Date_____ Grade: [ ] Pass [ ] Fail

Intended Outcome: Given a mouth mirror and soft bristle toothbrush, the student will perform the following tasks with 100% accuracy.

	Tasks	Clinical/Laboratory	
		Pass	Fail
1.	Grasp the toothbrush with a firm grip and utilize a hand mirror to assess tooth brushing technique.		
2.	Begin on the maxillary buccal surfaces of the two most posterior teeth. Angle the toothbrush at a 45° angle to the long axis of the tooth.		
3.	Choosing no more than two teeth at a time, gently move the toothbrush against the teeth and gums using small vibratory strokes. Brush for a count of 10.		
4.	Continue around the mouth until all the buccal and facial surfaces have been brushed.		
5.	Begin on the maxillary lingual surfaces of the two most posterior teeth and continue until all the lingual surfaces have been brushed.		
6.	Begin on the mandibular quadrant on the buccal surfaces of the two most posterior teeth. Angle the toothbrush at a 45° angle to the long axis of the tooth.		
7.	Choosing no more than two teeth at a time, gently move the toothbrush against the teeth and gums using small vibratory strokes. Brush for a count of 10.		
8.	Continue around the mouth until all the buccal and facial tooth surfaces have been brushed.		
9.	Continue on the mandibular lingual surfaces of the two most posterior teeth and continue until all the lingual surfaces have been brushed.		
10.	Begin on the furthermost tooth in a maxillary quadrant. Place the bristles on the chewing surface of the teeth and use a back-and-forth motion across the occlusal surfaces. Brush from the furthermost tooth toward the premolars for a count of 10.		
11.	Continue until all the occlusal surfaces have been brushed.		
12.	Rinse to remove plaque and debris.		
Comments			

3.0 FLOSSING PROCEDURE

Student Name:_____

Lab Evaluator:_____Date_____ Grade: [ ] Pass [ ] Fail

CL Evaluator:_____Date_____ Grade: [ ] Pass [ ] Fail

Intended Outcome: Using waxed or unwaxed dental floss, a hand mirror, and the assistance of a partner, the student will perform the following tasks on themselves with 100% accuracy.

	Tasks	Clinical/Laboratory	
		Pass	Fail
1.	Your partner will hold the hand mirror while you practice. Remove a piece of floss approximately 18 inches long.		
2.	Wrap the ends of the floss around your middle fingers until the length of the floss is approximately two inches. Use your other fingers to help guide the floss.		
3.	Beginning on the most posterior interproximal surface of a mandibular or maxillary tooth, glide the floss between the teeth using a back-and-forth motion. Avoid snapping the floss against the gum tissue.		
4.	Curve the floss in a C-shape around the tooth. Guide the floss into the sulcus maintaining a C-shape. Gently floss the area four to five times using an up and down motion.		
5.	Remove the floss from the sulcus area and curve the floss in a C-shape around the opposing tooth. Glide the floss into the sulcus, maintaining a C-shape. Gently floss the area four to five ties using an up and down motion.		
6.	Remove the floss from the contact area with an upward gliding motion. Unwrap the floss from the fingers and wrap a new section of unused floss around the same fingers. Proceed to the next interproximal area.		
7.	Continue in this manner until all the interproximal surfaces have been flossed.		
Comments			

4.0 VITAL SIGNS PROCEDURE

Student Name:_____

Lab Evaluator:_____Date_____ Grade: [ ] Pass [ ] Fail

CL Evaluator:_____Date_____ Grade: [ ] Pass [ ] Fail

Intended Outcome: Given the knowledge of vital statistics, a sphygmomanometer, a stethoscope, a thermometer, a timepiece, a chart, a writing instrument, and a patient, the student will perform the following tasks with 100% accuracy.

	Tasks	Clinical/Laboratory	
		Pass	Fail
1.	Have the patient bare an arm without obstruction up to the shoulder.		
2.	Place the sphygmomanometer around the upper arm between the shoulder and the elbow, with the pressure gauge tubing lined up over the medial aspect of the antecubital fossa.		
3.	Place the earpieces of the stethoscope in the ears and the tympanic piece over the brachial artery in the antecubital fossa.		
4.	Inflate the cuff until there is not a pulse sound appreciated through the stethoscope. (Usually 160 to 180)		
5.	As pressure is released from the cuff, record the pressure reading on the gauge for when you first hear a pulse sound then again when the pulse sound is no longer heard.		
6.	Place the pads of the index and middle fingers on the inner surface of the patient's wrist (between the radius and the tendon). Start counting with 0 for the first pulse; the next pulse felt will be counted as 1 and so on. Count the pulse for thirty seconds and then multiply by 2 to complete the rate for one full minute.		
7.	Using a timepiece and watching the patient, count the number of breaths taken in a 20 second period, multiply this number by three, and then record the number.		
Comments			

5.0   PERSONAL PROTECTIVE EQUIPMENT PROCEDURE

Student Name:_____

Lab Evaluator:_____Date_____ Grade: [ ] Pass [ ] Fail

CL Evaluator:_____Date_____ Grade: [ ] Pass [ ] Fail

Intended Outcome: Given the necessary personal supplies (lab jacket, gloves, masks, and goggles) to don and take off personal protective equipment, the student will perform the following tasks with 100% accuracy.

	Tasks	Clinical/Laboratory	
		Pass	Fail
Don Personal Protective Equipment			
1.	Put on fresh lab jacket and fasten properly		
2.	Put on protective eyewear.		
3.	Placed mask on face and fasten properly, adjust nose area to fit snugly.		
4.	Wash and dry hands, then put on exam gloves.		
5.	Tuck cuff of sleeves into the gloves.		
Removing Personal Protective Equipment			
1.	Grasp the cuff of the first glove and pull it off turning it inside out. As you do, keep this glove in the gloved hand.		
2.	With the ungloved hand, grasp the inside of the cuff of the other glove, pull the glove off turning it inside out, keeping the first glove inside. Throw the gloves in the proper waste receptacle.		
3.	Grasp the elastic or ties of the mask and remove it from the face, being cautious not to touch the contaminated front area. Throw the mask away.		
4.	Grasp the protective eyewear by the earpiece and remove from the face. Place by sink to clean and disinfect.		
5.	Remove the lab jacket and place in the proper area.		
6.	Wash hands.		
Comments			

6.0   DISCLOSING PROCEDURE

Student Name:_____

Lab Evaluator:_____Date_____ Grade: [ ] Pass [ ] Fail

CL Evaluator:_____Date_____ Grade: [ ] Pass [ ] Fail

Intended Outcome: Given the knowledge of dental anatomy, eighteen (18) developed radiographs, a mount, table surface, and a light source, the student will be able to perform the following tasks with 100% accuracy.

	Tasks	Clinical/Laboratory	
		Pass	Fail
1.	Arrange all dental films with dimples facing up from table top.		
2.	Group bitewings, anterior periapicals, and posterior periapicals.		
3.	Separate maxillary from mandibular periapicals.		
4.	Separate all films left and right. (Note: With the dimple facing toward the reader, identify the teeth in the radiograph and place with teeth anteriorly to center of the mount.		
5.	Insert each film into the appropriate slot on the x-ray mount (dimple facing up).		
6.	Label the mounts with patient name and date.		
Comments			

7.0   ACRYLIC DISK POLISHING PROCEDURE

Student Name:_____

Lab Evaluator:_____Date_____ Grade: [ ] Pass [ ] Fail

CL Evaluator:_____Date_____ Grade: [ ] Pass [ ] Fail

Intended Outcome: Given the necessary didactic instruction, supplies, and equipment to perform polishing acrylic, the student will perform the following tasks on an acrylic disk with imperfections with 100% accuracy.

	Tasks	Clinical/Laboratory	
		Pass	Fail
1.	Assemble acrylic disk polishing tray set up. Gloves Eyewear Acrylic disk Lathe Arbor band or latch-type acrylic bur Slow speed handpiece Wet-rag wheel Medium grit pumice Flour of pumice		
2.	Take required safety precautions.		
3.	Reduce the bulk with the arbor band on the lathe or an acrylic bur in the handpiece.		
4.	Refine surface with an acrylic bur in the handpiece.		
5.	Polish on low with a wet-rag wheel and medium pumice.		
6.	Polish on low with a wet-rag wheel and flour of pumice.		
7.	Rinse and evaluate disk.		
Comments			

8.0   DIAGNOSTIC CAST PROCEDURE

Student Name:_____

Lab Evaluator:_____Date_____ Grade: [ ] Pass [ ] Fail

CL Evaluator:_____Date_____ Grade: [ ] Pass [ ] Fail

Intended Outcome: Given the necessary diagnostic casting equipment and supplies, the student will perform the following tasks with 100% accuracy.

	Tasks	Clinical/Laboratory	
		Pass	Fail
	Set up the workstation by assembling the following 12 materials:		
	Flexible mixing bowl		
	Large mixing spatula		
	Small mixing spatula		
	Vibrator		
	Dental model plaster		
	Rubber model base formers		
	Maxillary stock tray to fit the typodontal model		
	Mandibular stock tray to fit the typodontal model		
	Sink for water and hand washing		
	Paper towels		
	Gloves		
	Produce a diagnostic model of the dental arches by performing the following 20 tasks:		
1.	Wash, dry, and glove hands.		
2.	Select a tray that will fit the typodont model provided.		
3.	Measure out the alginate powder.		
4.	Measure out the correct amount of water.		
5.	Pour the alginate into the mixing bowl.		
6.	Pour the water into the mixing bowl.		
7.	Mix the material until the mix is creamy, remembering to keep the amount of air incorporation to a minimum to prevent bubble formation.		
8.	Load the mandibular tray.		
9.	Place the loaded tray onto the mandibular teeth of the typodont in a manner that simulates insertion into an actual patient's mouth. This must be done remembering to seat the posterior section of the tray first and then rocking it onto the anterior teeth.		
10.	Once the material is set, the student will remove the impression from the typodont and repeat the procedures for the upper arch.		
11.	Have the instructor check the impressions to ensure all the teeth are registered without excessive show-through on the occlusal, that the extensions of the impressions are appropriate, and that all the teeth are properly registered.		

	Tasks	Clinical/Laboratory	
		Pass	Fail
12.	Proceed to pour-up the impressions by measuring the dental plaster into the flexible bowl.		
13.	Measure out the correct amount of water and pour it into the mixing bowl.		
14.	Mix the material with the intention of preventing a lot of air incorporation and use the vibrator to eliminate as much of the incorporated air as possible from the mix. Determine correct consistency.		
15.	Pour the impressions by dipping a small amount of plaster out of the mix with a mixing spatula and running the mixture into the impression from one point using the vibrator to help the material slowly advance to each of the teeth and other features of the impression.		
16.	Lay the poured impression aside for a moment while a sufficient quantity of the mixed plaster is loaded into the rubber base former.		
17.	Invert the poured impression over the base former and seat without embedding the tray itself in the plaster.		
18.	Repeat the procedures with the other impression.		
19.	Once the plaster is set (45-60 minutes), remove the impressions from the new model without breaking teeth.		
20.	Have the instructor inspect the study model for acceptability.		
Comments			

9.0 TREATMENT ROOM BREAKDOWN PROCEDURE

Student Name:_____

Lab Evaluator:_____Date_____ Grade: [ ] Pass [ ] Fail

CL Evaluator:_____Date_____ Grade: [ ] Pass [ ] Fail

Intended Outcome: Given the necessary didactic instruction, supplies, and equipment to breakdown a dental treatment room, the student will perform the following tasks with 100% accuracy.

	Tasks	Clinical/Laboratory Pass	Clinical/Laboratory Fail
1.	Remove mask and gloves following completion of the dental procedure. Leave safety glasses on.		
2.	Complete chart entry.		
3.	Walk patient out to the front desk.		
4.	Return to treatment room.		
5.	Put on utility gloves.		
6.	Clear tray of disposables.		
7.	Place items into the biobag at the unit.		
8.	Run handpieces for 30 seconds.		
9.	Remove handpieces and place on tray.		
10.	Strip barriers off of chair, stools, cart, and light.		
11.	Wipe handpieces, HVE, a/w syringes with disinfectant.		
12.	Lay handpieces, HVE, syringes on a paper towel and spray them with an acceptable disinfectant.		
13.	Take tray of contaminated items to the sterilization area and separate.		
14.	Remove the barrier from the instrument tray.		
15.	Return to the treatment room, remove glasses, spray with disinfectant.		
16.	Spray utility gloves with disinfectant.		
17.	Wash hands.		
Comments			

DENTAL FUNDAMENTALS

CONTENTS

DENTAL FUNDAMENTALS

A knowledge of dental fundamentals is essential to the dental assistant. You will use this knowledge every day, when you complete dental records and other related forms, and when you assist the dental officer in treating a patient.

The first section of this chapter deals with the anatomy of the head and neck. When you complete the section, you should be able to identify the major bones of the cranium and face, the anatomical landmarks of the maxillae and the mandible, the muscles of mastication, and the structures of the respiratory system located in the head and neck. The second section of the chapter covers dental anatomy, providing a description of the external features of the teeth. When you finish the section, you should be able to identify these features and classify each tooth by name, location, and number. Upon completing the final section,

"Dental Histology," you should be able to identify the tissues of the teeth and their supporting structures.

This chapter contains many new, unfamiliar words. Therefore, when you read the chapter, you may want to refer to

a glossary that defines some commonly used medical and dental terms. You should become familiar with such terms.

1. ANATOMY OF THE HEAD AND NECK

The dental assistant is concerned not only with the teeth themselves, but also with their surrounding tissues and supporting structures. The major bones of the skull form supporting structures for the teeth and provide attachments for many of the muscles responsible for the masticatory (chewing) process. Some of these bones actually form the sockets in which the teeth are embedded. The skull is composed of cranial bones and facial bones.

CRANIAL BONES

The cranium, which encases and protects the brain, consists of eight bones: the frontal bone, two temporal bones, two parietal bones, the occipital bone, the sphenoid bone, and the ethmoid bone (figs. 1 and 2). The sphenoid and ethmoid bones are not important to the present study, so they are not discussed here, nor are they shown in the figures.

The frontal bone forms the forehead, part of the roof of the eye sockets, and part of the nasal cavity. The frontal sinuses (air spaces in the bone) are located above each eye socket.

One temporal bone is located on each side of the skull. These bones form part of the sides and the base of the skull in the area of the ears. The bones house the hearing organs.

The two parietal bones are located posteriorly to (behind) the frontal bone. The parietal bones form the greater part of the roof and the sides of the skull.

The occipital bone forms the back and part of the base of the skull. There is a large foramen, or opening, in this bone through which the spinal cord passes.

FACIAL BONES

The facial bones include two each of the following: the nasal bones, the inferior nasal conchae, the lacrimal bones, the zygomatic bones, the palatine bones, and the maxillae; in addition, there is one vomer and one mandible (figs. 1 and 2). Some of these bones—the lacrimal bones, the inferior nasal conchae, and the vomer—are unimportant to the present study, so they are not discussed here, nor are they shown in the figures.

The nasal bones are small and oblong. They are located side by side at the middle and upper part of the nose. When they are joined, these bones form the upper part of the bridge of the nose.

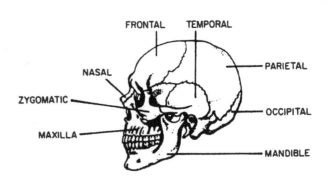

Figure 1.—The skull, side view.

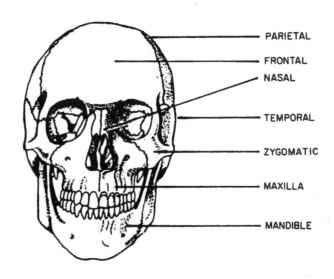

Figure 2.—The skull, front view.

The zygomatic bones, or "cheekbones," form the prominent part of the cheek under each eye.

The palatine bones form the right and left posterior portions of the palate, or roof of the mouth (fig. 3). They also contribute to the formation of the floor and the outer walls of the nasal cavity.

Of all the facial bones, the most important for dentistry are the maxillae and the mandible. Following is a discussion of the major features (landmarks) of these facial bones.

DENTAL FUNDAMENTALS

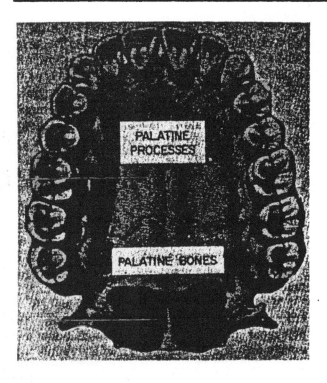

Figure 3.--The palate, showing the palatine bones and the palatine processes.

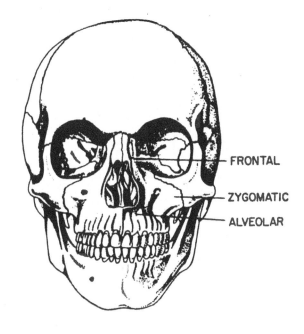

FRONTAL

ZYGOMATIC

ALVEOLAR

Figure 4.--The frontal, zygomatic, and alveolar processes of the maxilla.

Landmarks of the Maxillae

The maxillae (plural, maxilla is singular) are two facial bones that unite to form the upper jaw. Each maxilla contributes to the formation of the boundaries of the roof of the mouth, the floor and the outer walls of the nose, and the floor of each eye socket.

Each maxilla has a body and four processes. The body is shaped like a pyramid, and within the walls of the body is a large cavity--the maxillary sinus--which is the largest sinus in the skull. The four processes located on each maxilla are the frontal, zygomatic, alveolar, and palatine (figs. 3 and 4).

The frontal process extends upward and backward along the side of the nose. The zygomatic process joins the zygomatic bone to form the zygomatic arch, which makes up the foundation of the cheek. The alveolar process extends downward from the body of each maxilla to provide eight deep sockets into which fit the roots of teeth. When the right and left maxillae are united, the alveolar processes form the maxillary arch. The palatine processes unite to form the roof of the mouth and the anterior (front) portion of the floor of the nasal cavity.

Landmarks of the Mandible

The mandible, or lower jawbone, is a single bone consisting of a horizontal body, curved somewhat in the manner of a horseshoe, and two rami (plural, ramus is singular) that rise perpendicular to the body (fig. 5). The alveolar process of the mandible, like the alveolar processes of the maxillae, contains sockets for the roots of teeth.

The upper border of each ramus presents two distinct features: the coronoid process and the condyloid process. The coronoid process is the anterior projection of each ramus. It serves as an attachment for the muscle that raises the mandible. The condyloid process, or condyle, is the posterior projection of each ramus. It forms a hinge joint with a socket in the temporal bone. This joint is referred to as the temporomandibular joint. It is because of this joint that the mandible is able to move independently of the maxillae.

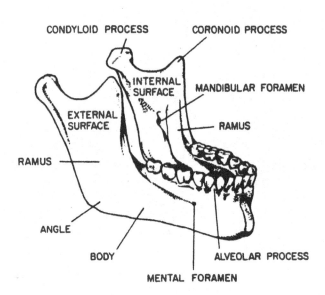

CONDYLOID PROCESS

CORONOID PROCESS

INTERNAL SURFACE

MANDIBULAR FORAMEN

EXTERNAL SURFACE

RAMUS

RAMUS

ANGLE

BODY

ALVEOLAR PROCESS

MENTAL FORAMEN

Figure 5.—The mandible.

On the internal surface of each ramus is the mandibular foramen, which provides an entrance for blood vessels and nerves. The nerves and blood vessels continue through the body of the mandible, exiting on the external surface of the mandible at the mental foramen (one is located on each side of the mandible). At the lower junction of the body and the ramus is located the angle of the mandible.

MUSCLES OF MASTICATION

The movement of the mandible is controlled by four pairs of muscles: the masseter, temporalis, medial pterygoid, and lateral pterygoid muscles. Taken together, these four pairs of muscles are known as the major muscles of mastication. Each of these major muscles of mastication will be discussed in terms of origin, insertion, and action.

Each muscle has two ends. One end is called the origin, the other the insertion. The origin is the end of the muscle that is attached to a relatively fixed part of the skeleton; thus, the origin remains more or less stationary when the muscle contracts. The insertion, on the other hand, is the end of the muscle that is attached to

a more movable part of the skeleton; thus, the insertion shows more movement than the origin when the muscle contracts. The action of a muscle is the movement of organs or parts of the body produced by the muscle when it contracts.

Masseter muscle:—This is a flat, thick muscle that originates along the zygomatic arch and inserts into the lateral surfaces of the angle and ramus of the mandible (fig. 6). The action of the muscle is to raise the mandible and close the mouth.

Temporalis muscle:—This is a large, fan-shaped muscle that originates along the temporal bone and inserts into the coronoid process of the mandible (fig. 6). The action of this muscle is to assist the masseter muscle in raising the mandible and closing the mouth.

Medial pterygoid muscle:—This is a triheaded muscle that originates on the pterygoid process of the sphenoid bone and inserts into the medial surface of the ramus (fig. 7). The action of the muscle is to raise the mandible and close the mouth.

Lateral pterygoid muscle:—This is a biheaded muscle that originates on the pterygoid process of the sphenoid bone and inserts into the

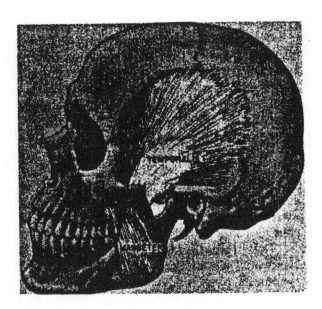

Figure 6.—Masseter and temporalis muscles.

DENTAL FUNDAMENTALS

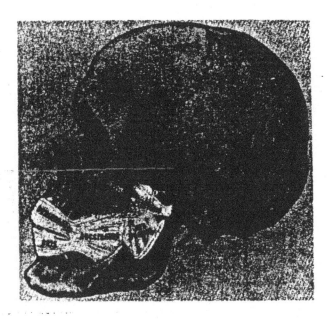

Figure 7.—Medial and lateral pterygoid, buccinator, and orbicularis oris muscles.

Figure 8.—The mylohyoid muscle.

condyloid process of the mandible (fig. 7). In mastication, this muscle acts to protrude or depress the mandible (open the mouth).

Acting independently, but always in association with the major muscles of mastication, are several accessory muscles of mastication. The buccinator muscle forms the cheek, and the orbicularis oris muscle forms the lips (fig. 7). The mylohyoid muscle forms the floor of the mouth under the tongue (fig. 8). The tongue itself is a muscular organ that moves food around in the mouth and aids in mastication.

STRUCTURES OF THE RESPIRATORY SYSTEM

Respiration (breathing) is one of the vital functions of the body. The dental assistant should have a basic understanding of the respiratory structures, since he may be required to perform emergency resuscitative procedures in the dental operatory.

Respiration causes air to be drawn into and expelled from the lungs. Respiration provides oxygen for the body tissues and serves as the main exhaust for carbon dioxide. The following paragraphs describe the path of the air as it enters the nose and mouth until it passes into the lungs, where a transfer of oxygen and carbon dioxide takes place. Figure 9 shows the major respiratory structures involved in this process.

The air enters the nasal cavity through the nostrils. Lining the nasal passages are tiny hairs called cilia. These hairs, along with mucous membranes, trap and filter out dust and other minute particles of foreign matter. In the chambers of the nasal cavity, the air is warmed and moistened. The air then passes through the pharynx, which is the upper part of the throat. The pharynx is a passageway for both food and air; it also filters the air before the air goes any farther.

The air next passes through the larynx, or "voice box," which is located between the base of the tongue and the trachea. It is here that the vocal cords are found. The larynx is covered by a flap of tissue, the epiglottis. When a person swallows, the epiglottis covers the entrance of the larynx, preventing foods or liquids from entering the trachea. After the air has passed through the larynx, it enters the trachea, or windpipe. The trachea is a tube lined with cilia and mucous membranes for filtration. The trachea carries the air to the lungs, where the transfer of oxygen and carbon dioxide occurs.

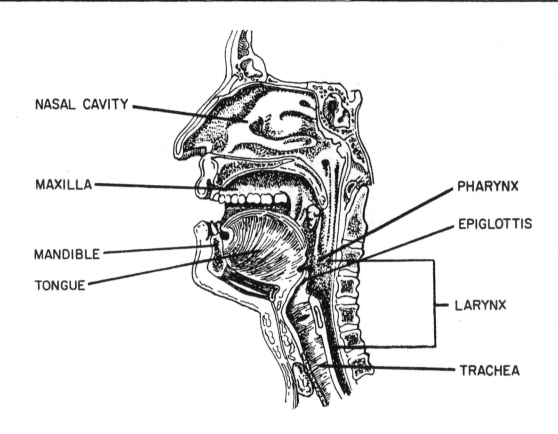

Figure 9.—Structures of the respiratory system.

2 . DENTAL ANATOMY

Dental anatomy deals with the external features of the teeth. To understand the material in this section, you must become familiar with the terms used to describe the external features of the teeth. To perform your duties efficiently and completely, you must know the full name, the location, and the anatomy of each tooth in the mouth. In addition, you must know the numbering system by which the teeth are identified on the standard dental chart used by the armed services. Such knowledge will be useful to you throughout your career, when you fill in dental charts, expose radiographs, clean teeth, and assist in all phases of dentistry.

In the discussion that follows, keep in mind that teeth differ in size, shape, and other characteristics from one person to another. This discussion concentrates on the most commonly observed external features of the teeth.

FUNCTIONS OF THE TEETH

Each tooth in the mouth can be classified as either an incisor, a cuspid, a bicuspid, or a molar (fig. 10). Each type of tooth performs a particular function in the masticatory process. The incisors have edges for cutting food. The cuspids and bicuspids have points (cusps) for grasping and tearing food. The molars have broad chewing surfaces for grinding solid masses of food.

LOCATION OF THE TEETH

Normally, the adult human gets two sets of teeth during his lifetime. The first (deciduous) set consists of 20 teeth. The second (permanent) set usually consists of 32 teeth. Half of the teeth are located in the maxillary arch, embedded in the alveolar processes of the maxillae. These are the maxillary teeth. The remaining half of the teeth are located in the mandibular arch,

DENTAL FUNDAMENTALS

INCISOR   CUSPID   BICUSPID   MOLAR

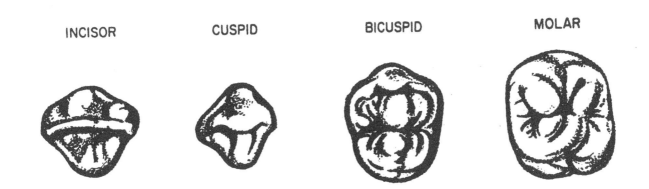

Figure 10.—Types of human teeth.

embedded in the alveolar process of the mandible. These are the mandibular teeth.

The mouth is divided into two arches, the maxillary arch and the mandibular arch. Each arch, in turn, is divided into a right and a left quadrant. The quadrants are formed by an imaginary line called the midline, or median line, that passes between the central incisors in each arch and divides the arch in half (fig. 11). There are four quadrants in the mouth (two per arch), and they divide the mouth into four equal parts. (Quadrant means "one fourth," and each quadrant is one fourth of the entire mouth.) Teeth are described as being located in one of the four quadrants: the right maxillary quadrant, the left maxillary quadrant, the right mandibular quadrant, or the left mandibular quadrant.

In each quadrant, there are eight permanent teeth: two incisors, one cuspid, two bicuspids, and three molars (fig. 12). The tooth positioned immediately to the side of the midline is the central incisor, so called because it occupies a central location in the arch. To the side of the central incisor is the lateral incisor. Next is the cuspid, then the two bicuspids (the first bicuspid, followed by the second bicuspid). The last teeth are the molars. There are three molars. After the second bicuspid comes the first molar, followed by the second molar, followed by the third molar (the "wisdom tooth").

Another, but less exact, method of describing the location of the teeth is to refer to them as anterior or posterior teeth (fig. 12). Anterior teeth are those located in the front of the mouth, the incisors and the cuspids. Normally, these are the teeth that are visible when a person smiles. The posterior teeth are those located in the back of the mouth, the bicuspids and the molars.

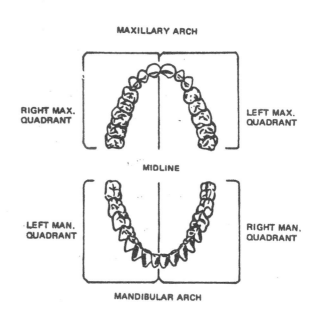

Figure 11.—Maxillary and mandibular arches divided into quadrants.

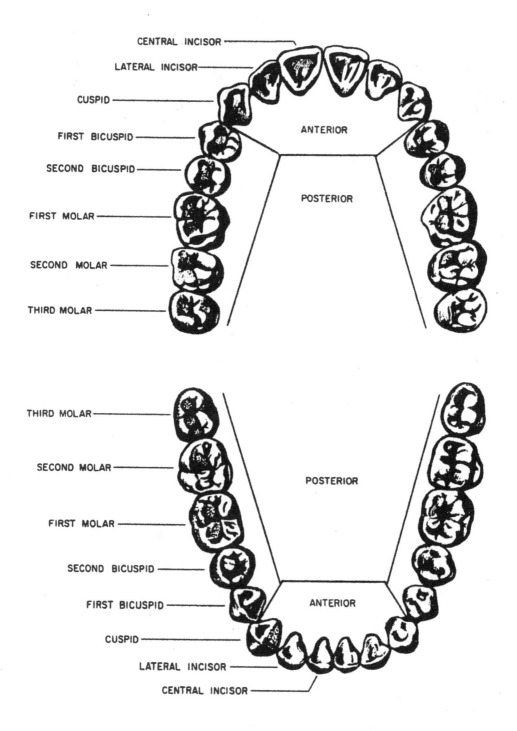

Figure 12.—Names of the teeth in the right maxillary and mandibular quadrants; anterior and posterior teeth.

DENTAL FUNDAMENTALS

IDENTIFICATION OF THE TEETH

In order to avoid confusion, you must identify a tooth as completely as possible. Give its full name: central incisor (not just incisor), second molar (not just molar), etc. But even the full name of a tooth does not provide adequate identification, since there are several teeth with the same name. Complete tooth identification requires that you identify the quadrant in which the tooth appears, in addition to giving the full name of the tooth. Therefore, you would identify a specific second molar in the following manner: right mandibular second molar. Although there are four second molars in the mouth, naming the quadrant (right

mandibular) narrows the field down to one specific second molar.

There is a simplified method of identifying the teeth. This method employs numbers, with each tooth designated by a separate number from 1 to 32. Although there are several accepted numbering systems, only the one used by the armed services will be explained here. Figure 13 shows the numbering system employed on the standard dental chart. When charting, you would refer to a tooth by number rather than name. Instead of referring to the right maxillary third molar, you would refer to tooth No. 1. Each tooth has its own number. If any tooth is missing from the mouth, always leave a space for it when counting the teeth. For example, if the

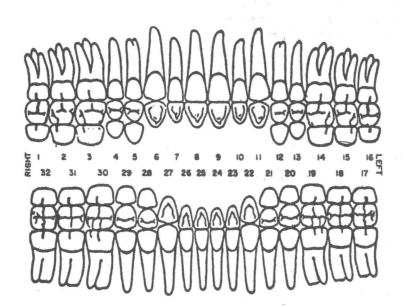

1. Right maxillary third molar.
2. Right maxillary second molar.
3. Right maxillary first molar.
4. Right maxillary second bicuspid.
5. Right maxillary first bicuspid.
6. Right maxillary cuspid.
7. Right maxillary lateral incisor.
8. Right maxillary central incisor.
9. Left maxillary central incisor.
10. Left maxillary lateral incisor.
11. Left maxillary cuspid.
12. Left maxillary first bicuspid.
13. Left maxillary second bicuspid.
14. Left maxillary first molar.
15. Left maxillary second molar.
16. Left maxillary third molar.
17. Left mandibular third molar.
18. Left mandibular second molar.
19. Left mandibular first molar.
20. Left mandibular second bicuspid.
21. Left mandibular first bicuspid.
22. Left mandibular cuspid.
23. Left mandibular lateral incisor.
24. Left mandibular central incisor.
25. Right mandibular central incisor.
26. Right mandibular lateral incisor.
27. Right mandibular cuspid.
28. Right mandibular first bicuspid.
29. Right mandibular second bicuspid.
30. Right mandibular first molar.
31. Right mandibular second molar.
32. Right mandibular third molar.

Figure 13.—Standard dental chart; names and numbers of the teeth.

right maxillary second molar (No. 2) is missing, the right maxillary first molar still remains tooth No. 3, the right maxillary second bicuspid No. 4, and so on. Failure to follow this procedure will cause confusion and result in misnumbering the teeth.

When using the standard dental chart, remember that the right and left sides are reversed. The right side of a patient's mouth appears on the left side of the dental chart; the left side of a patient's mouth appears on the right side of the dental chart. (The directional terms "left" and "right" are printed on the chart to avoid confusion.) This arrangement is necessary because the dental officer and the assistant see the sides reversed when they look into a patient's mouth.

SURFACES OF THE TEETH

Not only must the assistant be able to name and locate a tooth, but he must also be able to identify a specific tooth surface. Figure 14 shows a number of the different surfaces of the teeth.

The facial surface is the outer surface of a tooth adjacent to the lips and the cheeks. The facial surface of an anterior tooth is often referred to as the labial surface because it lies next to the labia, or lips. The facial surface of a posterior tooth is often referred to as the buccal surface because it lies next to the buccinator, or cheek, muscle.

The lingual surface is the surface of an anterior or posterior tooth that faces toward the tongue.

The mesial surface is the surface of a tooth that, following the curvature of the dental arch, is closest to or facing the midline of the arch.

Distal is the opposite of mesial. The distal surface is the tooth surface that, following the curvature of the dental arch, faces away from the midline.

Incisal edges are narrow cutting edges found only on the anterior teeth (incisors and cuspids). Incisors have one incisal edge. Cuspids have two incisal edges that meet at the tip of the cusp.

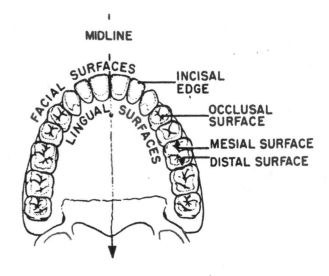

Figure 14.—Surfaces of the teeth.

The occlusal surface is the broad chewing surface found on posterior teeth (bicuspids and molars).

To get a clearer picture of the various tooth surfaces, refer to figure 13, which has previously been discussed. The standard dental chart shows each of the teeth "unfolded," so that the facial, occlusal or incisal, and lingual surfaces of the teeth can be shown. For the posterior teeth, the facial surfaces are shown adjacent to the roots, followed by the occlusal surfaces, and then by the lingual surfaces (which are located next to the numbers on the chart). For the anterior teeth, the facial surfaces are shown adjacent to the roots, and the incisal edges are shown as a line between the facial and lingual surfaces. The lingual surfaces are located next to the numbers on the chart.

Tooth surfaces that face each other are called proximal surfaces (fig. 15). The proximal surface includes the entire length of the tooth from the crown to the root tip. The point on proximal surfaces where two teeth actually touch each other is the contact point. The area between the teeth is referred to as the interproximal space. Part of the interproximal space is occupied by the interdental papilla (singular, papillae is plural). The interdental papilla is a triangular fold of gingival tissue. The

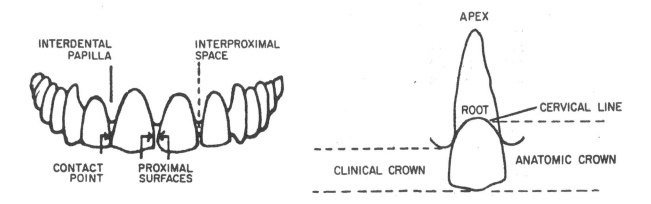

Figure 15.—Adjacent tooth surfaces and spaces.

Figure 17.—Tooth crown and root.

part of the interproximal space not occupied by the interdental papilla is called the embrasure. The embrasure occupies an area bordered by the interdental papilla, the proximal surfaces of two adjacent teeth, and the contact point (fig. 16). If there is no contact point between the teeth, then the area between them is called a diastema instead of an embrasure.

ANATOMICAL LANDMARKS

Every tooth has a crown and a root portion (fig. 17). The crown is divided into the

anatomic crown and the clinical crown. The anatomic crown is the part of the tooth that is covered with enamel. The clinical crown is the part of the tooth that is exposed (visible) in the mouth. The cervical line, or cervix, is a slight indentation that encircles the tooth and marks the junction of the crown with the root. The tip of each root is called the apex. On the apex of each root, there is a small opening that allows for the passage of blood vessels and nerves into the tooth. This opening is called the apical foramen.

A tooth may have a single root or it may have two, three, or more. When a tooth has two roots, the root portion is said to be bifurcated. When it has three roots, the root portion is said to be trifurcated (fig. 18). If a tooth has four or more roots, it is said to be multirooted. As a general rule, maxillary molars have three roots

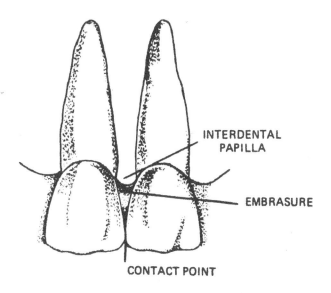

Figure 16.—Embrasure.

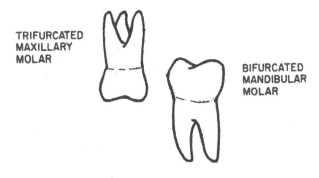

Figure 18.—Trifurcated and bifurcated roots.

and mandibular molars have two roots. Most bicuspids are single rooted, although approximately 50 percent of maxillary first bicuspids are bifurcated at the apex. Anterior teeth are single rooted.

A cusp is a rounded point on the working surface of a cuspid, bicuspid, or molar. A cuspid has a single cusp, a bicuspid has two, and a molar has four (sometimes five) cusps. If a fifth cusp is found, it will be on a maxillary first molar, usually on the lingual surface of the mesiolingual cusp. This fifth cusp is called the cusp of Carabelli. Figure 19 shows the significant features of the occlusal surface of a maxillary first molar.

A ridge is a linear elevation on the surface of a tooth. Several different ridges can be found on a tooth. A marginal ridge is the elevation of enamel that forms the mesial and distal margins (edges) of a tooth. On posterior teeth, this ridge is on the occlusal surfaces; on anterior teeth, it can be found on the lingual surfaces. A transverse ridge is any ridge found on posterior teeth that crosses the occlusal surface between cusps. This ridge is not shown in figure 19; it is most prominent on maxillary bicuspids. An oblique ridge is found only on maxillary first and second molars. It crosses the occlusal surface diagonally from the distofacial cusp to the mesiolingual cusp. You should remember the location of this ridge. It is important for charting and for operative dentistry, since the dentist tries to preserve this strong ridge whenever possible.

A groove is a linear depression on the surface of a tooth. A marginal groove is a depression running perpendicular to a marginal ridge. Facial and lingual grooves are, simply, grooves on the facial and lingual surfaces of the teeth. Usually, they are extensions of a groove on the occlusal surface. The central groove is a depression passing from the mesial to the distal marginal ridges on the occlusal surface of a bicuspid. Grooves are indicated on the standard dental chart by means of dark lines (fig. 13).

A fossa is a shallow, irregular depression on the surface of a tooth. A pit is a small, definite pinpoint depression on the surface of a tooth. It is usually found at the bottom of a fossa, at the junction of two or more grooves, or at the end of a facial or lingual groove.

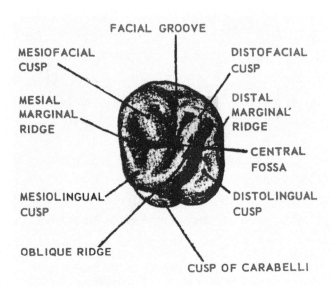

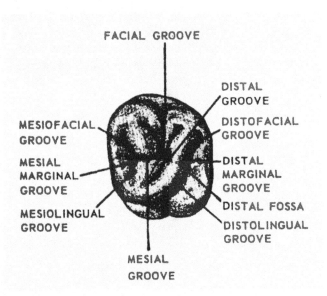

Figure 19.—Features of the occlusal surface of a maxillary first molar.

OCCLUSAL RELATIONSHIPS

Occlusion is the relationship between the occlusal surfaces of opposing maxillary and mandibular teeth when the teeth are in contact. When the mouth is closed and there is maximum contact between the occlusal surfaces of the mandibular and maxillary teeth, the position is

DENTAL FUNDAMENTALS

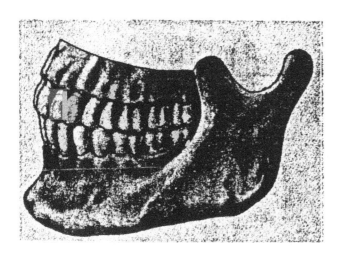

Figure 20.—Centric occlusion.

called centric occlusion (fig. 20). In normal jaw relations, when the teeth are of normal size and in the correct position, the mesiofacial cusp of the maxillary first molar fits into the facial groove of the mandibular first molar. This relationship between the two teeth is called the key to occlusion. The key to occlusion is clinical evidence of the correct relationship of the mandible to the maxillae.

The term "malocclusion" is used to describe any deviation from normal occlusion. Vertical overlap, or overbite, is a condition in which the vertical distance between the maxillary and mandibular incisal edges is abnormal when the other teeth are in normal occlusion (fig. 21).

Horizontal overlap, also called overjet or buck teeth, is a condition in which the horizontal distance between the maxillary and mandibular incisal edges is abnormal when the other teeth are in normal occlusion (fig. 21).

A prognathic maxillomandibular relationship is a condition in which there is a marked projection of the mandible, usually resulting in the lower teeth hitting anterior to the maxillary incisors (fig. 22). A retrognathic maxillomandibular relationship is a condition in which there is a marked recession of the mandible, producing a very receding chin (fig. 23).

3. DENTAL HISTOLOGY

Dental anatomy deals with the external form and appearance of the teeth. Dental histology

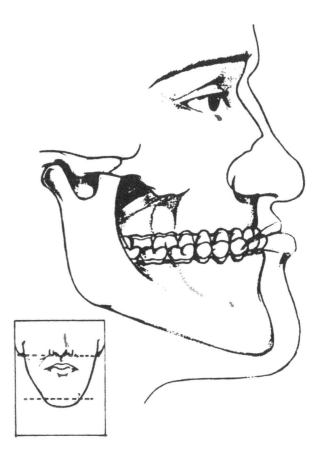

Figure 22.—Prognathic maxillomandibular relationship.

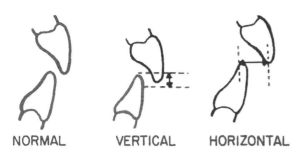

NORMAL   VERTICAL   HORIZONTAL

Figure 21.—Normal occlusion; vertical and horizontal overlap.

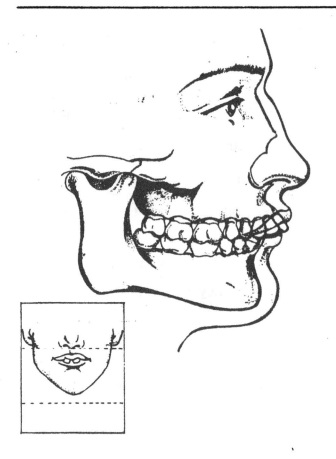

Figure 23.—Retrognathic maxillomandibular relationship.

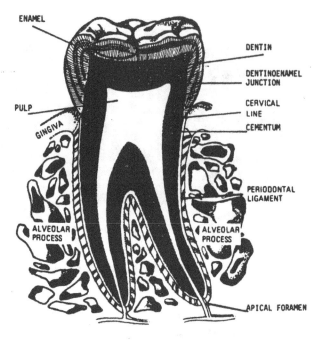

Figure 24.—The periodontium.

studies the tissues and internal structure of the teeth, along with the tissues that surround and support the teeth (tissues of the periodontium). A knowledge of dental histology will be of help to you when you mount radiographs, clean teeth, and provide emergency dental treatment.

TISSUES OF THE TEETH

Structurally, the teeth are composed of four different tissues: enamel, dentin, cementum, and pulp (fig. 24). Cementum is also considered a tissue of the periodontium, since it supports the teeth by providing attachment for the principal fibers of the periodontal ligament.

Enamel

Enamel is the calcified substance that covers the entire crown of the tooth. It consists of approximately 96 percent inorganic (nonliving) material, and it is the hardest tissue in the human body. Enamel is thickest at the cusps, thinning to a knife edge at the cervical line. The color of a tooth is derived from the enamel, which is usually shaded from light yellow to white.

Enamel is formed by cells called ameloblasts. Enamel is completely formed prior to tooth eruption, after which the ameloblasts become nonfunctional. This means that enamel is formed only once and cannot regenerate or repair itself. Thus, when enamel is destroyed by decay, operative dentistry is required to reconstruct the tooth. Enamel has no nerve fibers and cannot register sensations. It is strong and hard; it has the ability to withstand masticating forces; it resists abrasion or attrition; and it is thick in areas that contact opposing teeth. Because of these properties, enamel serves to protect the underlying softer dentin.

Dentin

Dentin is the light yellow substance that makes up the bulk of the tooth. Dentin is the

DENTAL FUNDAMENTALS

second hardest substance in the body. It is softer than enamel, but harder than bone. It consists of approximately 70 percent inorganic matter. It is slightly elastic and compressible.

Dentin is found inside the crown under the enamel. The point at which the dentin and the enamel meet is called the dentinoenamel junction. Dentin is also found inside the root of the tooth under the cementum. The inner surface of the dentin forms a hard-walled cavity that contains and protects the pulp.

Dentin is formed by cells called odontoblasts, which are part of the pulp. All of the dentin of a newly formed tooth is called primary dentin. Unlike enamel, dentin continues to form throughout the life of the tooth. When the dental pulp is mildly stimulated as a result of caries, cavity preparation, abrasion, attrition, or erosion, a protective layer of secondary dentin is formed on the pulp wall. When irritation is severe, irregular dentin is formed. Irregular dentin differs from secondary dentin only in that the irregular dentin is structurally weaker.

Even though dentin is not sensitive to stimuli, sensation may result when mechanical, thermal, or chemical stimuli are applied to the dentin. The sensation comes not from the dentin itself but from odontoblastic cells that extend into the dentin. These cells are actually part of the pulp, not the dentin, and they are sensitive to stimuli.

Cementum

Cementum is a bonelike substance, although it is not so hard as bone. It consists of approximately 50 percent inorganic material, and it forms a protective layer over the root portion of the dentin. The cementum joins the enamel at the cervix of the tooth. The point at which they join is called the cementoenamel junction (fig. 25). The cementum is thinnest at this junction. In most teeth, the cementum overlaps the enamel for a short distance. In some teeth, the cementum meets the enamel in a sharp line. In a few teeth, there is a break between the cementum and the enamel, exposing a narrow area of root dentin. Such areas are sensitive to thermal, chemical, or mechanical stimuli.

The main function of cementum is to anchor the tooth to the socket by providing attachment

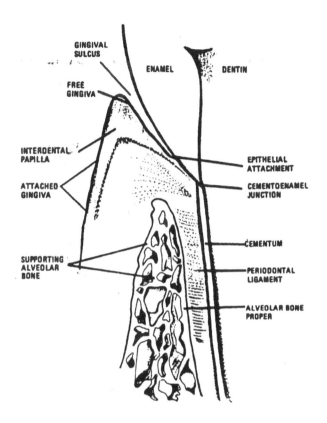

Figure 25.—Closeup view of the periodontium.

for the principal fibers of the periodontal ligament. (Additional information on this will be provided in the discussion of the periodontal ligament.) Cementum is formed continuously throughout the life of the tooth. Thus, it compensates for the loss of tooth substance due to occlusal wear, and it allows for the attachment of new fibers of the periodontal ligament to the root.

Pulp

The pulp is the soft tissue that fills the pulp cavity. This tissue contains numerous blood vessels and nerves which enter the tooth through the apical foramen. The pulp is enclosed within the hard, unyielding dentin walls of the pulp cavity. The pulp cavity has two parts: the pulp chamber and the root, or pulp, canal. The pulp chamber is located inside the crown. The root canal is located inside the root.

An important function of the pulp is the formation of dentin. The pulp provides the cells (odontoblasts) from which dentin is formed. The pulp also supplies the dentin with blood.

Pulp responds to external stimuli, providing sensation to the tooth. The pulp responds to irritation either by forming secondary dentin or by becoming inflamed. Since the walls of the pulp chamber and root canal permit no expansion of the pulp tissue, any inflammatory swelling of the tissue will compress the blood vessels against the walls. This results in a condition known as hyperemic pulp, which can lead to necrosis (death) of the pulp tissue.

TISSUES OF THE PERIODONTIUM

The tissues that surround and support the teeth are the cementum, the alveolar process, the periodontal ligament, and the gingiva. Collectively, these tissues are known as the periodontium. The cementum has been covered earlier, so it will not be discussed in this section. Throughout the following discussion, you should refer to figure 24 and to figure 25, which provides a closeup view of the periodontium.

Alveolar Process

The alveolar process is that portion of the maxillae and mandible that forms and supports the sockets (alveoli) of the teeth.

The alveolar process can be divided into two parts: the alveolar bone proper (or lamina dura) and the supporting alveolar bone. The alveolar bone proper is a thin layer of bone that lines the tooth socket and gives attachment to the principal fibers of the periodontal ligament. The supporting alveolar bone is the portion of the alveolar process that surrounds the alveolar bone proper and gives support to the tooth socket. The supporting alveolar bone is composed of inner and outer plates of compact bone (the cortical plates). Between these plates is found spongy, porous cancellous bone.

The quantity and quality of alveolar bone are affected by the amount of functional stress. If, because of tooth loss, a tooth in one arch does not make contact with any teeth in the opposing arch, the alveolar bone of the tooth socket will be under reduced stress and the bone will become much more rarefied (porous). When all the teeth are lost, the entire alveolar process undergoes partial atrophy.

Periodontal Ligament

The periodontal ligament consists of hundreds of tissue fibers that, except at the apical foramen, completely surround the root of the tooth. The ligament acts as a shock absorber, reducing the impact of the teeth as they occlude.

The periodontal ligament contains numerous bundles of fibers (principal fibers) that attach the tooth to the socket. These principal fibers are embedded on one side in the cementum of the tooth root and on the other side in the alveolar bone proper. In this manner, the tooth is suspended in the socket. Since the principal fibers are somewhat elastic, they permit a small amount of tooth movement. Also, the fibers are positioned so that the tooth can resist forces exerted upon it from all angles.

The periodontal ligament also supplies nutrition to the alveolar process. It supports and attaches the gingiva. It registers sensations of heat, cold, pressure, pain, and touch. Since the periodontal ligament can register such a wide range of sensations (as opposed to the pulp, which registers only pain), it is of special diagnostic importance to the dental officer.

The periodontal ligament varies in thickness according to the person, the location of the tooth, and the amount of tooth function. In dental radiographs, the ligament appears as a thin, dark line around the root. The alveolar bone proper appears as a thin, white line around the ligament.

Gingiva

The gingiva (singular, gingivae is plural) is the soft tissue that covers the alveolar process and surrounds the necks of the teeth. The gingiva consists of an outer layer of epithelium and an inner layer of connective tissue.

Depending upon whether or not it is attached to the tooth, the gingiva is described as being free or attached. The free gingiva is that portion of the gingiva surrounding the neck of the tooth just above the cervix, not directly

DENTAL FUNDAMENTALS

attached to the tooth, and forming the soft tissue wall of the gingival sulcus. The gingival sulcus is the V-shaped space between the free gingiva and the tooth. It extends to a depth of approximately 2 mm, at which point the gingiva is attached to the tooth by the epithelial attachment. The interdental papilla is the portion of the gingiva that fills the interproximal space between two adjacent teeth. It consists of both free and attached gingiva.

A healthy gingiva is pink, firm, and resilient. It has a stippled appearance. Stippling refers to the "orange peel" texture of the healthy tissue. Inflammation causes a loss of stippling. When inflamed, the gingiva may become sore and swollen, and it may bleed.

———

BASIC FUNDAMENTALS OF DENTAL MATERIALS

CONTENTS

BASIC FUNDAMENTALS OF DENTAL MATERIALS

Section I. INTRODUCTION

1. General

This chapter covers dental materials which are commonly handled or prepared by the dental specialist as part of his duties in assisting the dentist. The composition, properties, manipulation, and uses of these materials are discussed in this chapter. Dental materials which are peculiar, or which have greater application, to the dental laboratory and the work of the dental removable or fixed prosthetic specialists are discussed elsewhere.

2. Importance of Knowledge of Materials

The dental specialist may perform many procedures at the chair without having a comprehensive understanding of the materials being used. Yet he attains a far higher standard of accomplishment if he understands the nature and scientific composition of the materials, the reason for definite methods of manipulation, the results of improper handling or manipulation, and the reasons why faulty dental procedures result from such improper handling or manipulation. Our knowledge of materials used in dentistry is largely the result of continuing extensive scientific investigations. Specifications formulated for certain categories of dental materials and published by the American Dental Association serve to insure their suitability. Additional standards for quality are developed as further knowledge is gained. Optimum properties of dental materials can only be achieved through careful attention to details in their preparation and manipulation. Manufacturer's directions accompanying materials should be followed carefully. The techniques of manipulation discussed in this chapter are general and normally will give satisfactory results. However, if the manufacturer gives specific instructions regarding temperatures, mixing times, and ratios, they should be followed closely.

Section II. DENTAL SILVER ALLOY AND DENTAL AMALGAM

3. General

Silver and silver alloys mixed with mercury have been used more than a century for filling cavities in teeth. Little was known of the properties of the material or of how handling would affect them, so that early results of its uses were largely unsatisfactory and the materials fell into disfavor with the profession. About 1895 Dr. G. V. Black, often called the father of modem dentistry, began investigating the properties of amalgams. His studies showed the effects of chemical composition and physical structure on the properties of amalgam restorations. In 1919 the National Bureau of Standards began studies leading to the formulation of specifications for the selection and grading of dental amalgams, the first phase of a continuing extensive research program designed to improve dentistry through increased knowledge of the properties of dental materials. Due largely to the work done by Dr. Black, the National Bureau of Standards, and others, amalgam is used more than any other material for the restoration of posterior teeth.

4. Definition of Alloy and Amalgam

An alloy is a mixture of two or more metals. When mercury is one of the metals, the mixture is known as an amalgam. A dental amalgam is a combination of mercury with a specially prepared silver alloy for use as a dental restorative material. Amalgam is used also in making dies. In dentistry, a die is an exact, positive reproduction of an individual tooth and is used mainly for the fabrication of crowns, inlays, or fixed partial dentures.

5. Chemical Composition

Each metal incorporated into a dental silver alloy possesses specific properties when combined with mercury. Some properties are desirable and some are undesirable. An acceptable alloy is balanced so that the combined effects of the properties of its ingredients will provide the most satisfactory restorative material. Like other restorative materials, dental amalgam must meet the standards and requirements set by the National Bureau of Standards. The silver alloy composition, as well as the size of the fillings or shavings, varies slightly among manufacturers. Usually the silver alloy consists of silver and tin and perhaps other materials such as copper and zinc in limited amounts. Each manufacturer of silver alloy insures that his product meets the requirements of the National Bureau of Standards and American Dental Association. The composition of the alloy must include a minimum of 65 percent silver and 25 percent tin and must not contain more than 6 percent copper and 2 percent zinc. Some alloys are entirely zinc-free while others contain such additional materials as platinum or gold. The alloy is mixed with pure mercury, which is commonly known as "quicksilver" or "white liquid silver."

6. Physical Properties of Amalgam

The most important properties of amalgam are crushing strength, flow, and thermal conductivity.

a. *Crushing Strength.* The crushing strength of amalgam approaches 45,000 pounds per square inch (psi), which is completely acceptable when compared with other restorative materials and enamel and dentin. Enamel has a crushing strength of about 100,000 psi, dentin about 30,000 psi. These figures show amalgam to be an acceptable restorative material, even for restorations on stress-bearing areas of the teeth.

b. *Flow.* The amount of flow in amalgam is of a relatively low rate. Flow is the property of a material to flow or deform in shape when it is under stress or load for an extended time.

c. *Thermal Conductivity.* Thermal conductivity is the ability to transmit changes in temperature. Dental amalgam has a relatively high thermal conductivity. This becomes a distinct disadvantage when amalgam is placed close to the pulp. Amalgam allows heat or cold to pass through readily and irritate the pulp. To combat this disadvantage, an intermediate base with low thermal conductivity is placed under the amalgam.

7. Advantages and Disadvantages of Amalgam

a. Amalgam has many advantages over other materials for use as a restorative material. It is used more than any other material to restore carious teeth. It is easy to insert into the cavity preparation and adapts readily to cavity walls. In obtaining its initial set, or hardness, amalgam allows time for condensing and carving. It has an acceptable crushing strength and long life as a restoration. Before its final set, amalgam is easy to shape by carving.

b. Amalgam has several major disadvantages. First, its color does not match the color of teeth. It will tarnish with time no matter how well the amalgam restoration is prepared and inserted. To avoid or to reduce tarnish, the restoration is smoothed and highly polished a day or two after its insertion. The restoration may be reshined later at any time with little effort.

Because of its color, amalgam is used on the visible surfaces of anterior teeth only in exceptional circumstances. Another disadvantage is its inadequate edge strength. The edges of amalgam will fracture if unsupported by a bulk of amalgam. A third disadvantage of amalgam is its high thermal conductivity.

8. Elements and Their Effects on Amalgam

Each element composing amalgam imparts certain properties to the finished product. Silver imparts strength, durability, and color; gives the alloy desirable setting expansion; decreases flow; and accelerates the setting time. Tin makes the amalgam easier to work, controls excessive setting expansion, and increases both flow and setting time. Copper increases hardness, contributes to setting expansion, reduces flow, and decreases setting time. Zinc increases workability and cleanliness of the amalgam during trituration and condensation. Mercury, although an indispensable ingredient, imparts undesirable properties to the amalgam if added in incorrect proportions.

9. Setting Changes

The mixing of finely cut particles of silver alloy with mercury initiates the formation of a new alloy. Mixing (trituration) produces a soft mass in which all particles have been wetted with mercury. The mercury goes into solution with some of the particles of alloy and the hardening (setting) of amalgam is similar to the hardening process of the cements. Reactions which take place during hardening result in a cored structure consisting of a core of undisclosed alloy surrounded by a matrix of crystallized phases of the solution. As long as free mercury is present in excessive amounts, the amalgam will not set completely. For that reason, hardness of amalgam restorations is increased by eliminating as much excess mercury as possible during manipulation and placement of the material.

10. Properties Determined by the Manufacturer

a. Many factors controlled by the manufacturer influence the properties of dental silver alloys. Among them are purity of ingredients, proportioning of ingredients, controlled melting conditions, particle size, and proper heat treatment.

b. The effects of the ingredients upon the properties of a silver alloy were described in paragraph 8. Conditions under which these ingredients are melted to form the alloy must be controlled to prevent contamination through the introduction of oxides and other impurities. Particle size is important because as it decreases, the crushing strength of restorations made from the alloy is increased and setting expansion is reduced. Heat treatment to anneal (soften) the alloy after the formation of particles is essential to produce uniform crystalline structure of the material. When the metals composing a dental silver alloy are melted together and allowed to cool, the crystal composition of the alloy is subjected to tremendous strains. The molten mass solidifies or cools first on the outside. The crystals inside the mass, which solidify last, are of different composition. Thus the size of the crystals differs throughout the mass. To correct this, the alloy filings or shavings are annealed by heating slowly to 100°C (212°F). This method allows the crystalline structure to reorganize and produces an alloy of greater uniformity. This alloy requires less mercury for amalgamation and has less expansion and flow and greater crushing strength than the annealed material.

11. Properties Determined by the Operator

The following factors must be controlled by the dentist and his assistant to achieve satisfactory results.

a. Proper Ratio of Mercury to Alloy. The directions furnished by the manufacturer should be followed. These directions cover the proportions of alloy and mercury, trituration pressure, and trituration time. Too little mercury in a mix will produce a grainy, weak amalgam which is readily tarnished and corroded. Too much mercury in an amalgam restoration causes excessive expansion and weakens the material.

b. Proper Trituration. Both over trituration and under trituration are undesirable. Over trituration results in shorter setting time and increases shrinkage. Under trituration results in increased expansion, a lengthened setting time, and a weakened amalgam.

c. Proper Condensation. Condensation is the procedure of packing an amalgam mix by the dentist into a tooth cavity preparation. Time and pressure are important in achieving best results. Trituration of the amalgam should be so timed that the mix is ready at the exact time when the dentist desires to start the condensation. The longer the time between trituration and condensation is, the weaker the amalgam is, due to fracturing of forming crystals. Condensation should be completed in 3 1/2 minutes. Generally, the more pressure that is used, the stronger the restoration will be. Pressure of 8 to 10 pounds with a hand condenser is recommended.

d. Addition of Mercury. Addition of extra mercury should be avoided. If one drop of mercury is added to a partially set mix of average size, the compressive strength of the resulting amalgam will be about one-tenth of the normal strength. Once amalgam has begun to crystallize or harden, the addition of mercury lowers crushing strength tremendously.

e. Contamination by Moisture. Moisture should be avoided. Contact with any form of moisture contaminates freshly triturated amalgam. Moisture may cause excessive expansion, pain beginning several days after insertion of the restoration, lowered crushing strength, and blister formation on the amalgam surface. Moisture can be introduced into amalgam by mulling (working) the triturated amalgam in the palm of the hand, by trituration below the dew point (temperature at which moisture collects on a surface), by the presence of moisture in the cavity being filled, or by accidental contact with saliva. To avoid such contamination all instruments and equipment touching the amalgam should be dry. Mulling of amalgam should be done in a piece of rubber dam, a squeeze cloth, or a piece of clean linen but not in the palm of the hand. The temperature of equipment and materials should be kept high enough that no moisture collects. Saliva should be kept out of the cavity during insertion of the material. Amalgam that has accidentally contacted moisture in any form should be discarded.

12. Importance of Properly Mixed Amalgam

The dental specialist has the direct responsibility for the correct manipulation and preparation of amalgam for use as a restorative material. Incorrect manipulation may produce a faulty restoration which can cause or contribute to the loss of a tooth.

Therefore, the dental specialist must use extreme care in preparing a good mix of amalgam that will provide the best qualities obtainable from the alloy. Procedures in the manipulation of amalgam normally performed by dental specialists include proportioning the amounts of mercury to alloy; trituration to produce the amalgam; mulling; expressing free mercury; and assisting the dentist during insertion and condensation of the prepared amalgam.

13. Proportioning Alloy and Mercury

To proportion and mix dental alloy and mercury, the size of the mix and the alloy-mercury ratio must be known. The size of the mix is determined by the dentist. Dental alloy in pellets is the form used most in the restorative service of the dental clinic. The pellets are composed of silver alloy filings compressed under great pressure without a binding agent. They are supplied in weights ranging from 4.8 to 6 grains per pellet. A special dispenser is used to drop the pellets individually Pellets crush easily under light pressure of the pestle in a mortar or automatically by an amalgamator. Since the pellets are reformed in a set amount of silver alloy, only the amount of mercury used with each pellet needs to be measured. The mercury dispenser is equipped with four interchangeable plungers lettered A through D. The A plunger dispenses the most mercury; the D plunger the least. Changing the plunger allows for the individual preference of the dentist regarding the wetness or dryness of the amalgam when it is mixed. The manufacturer's instructions accompanying the pellets should be followed in selecting the size of plunger to use to provide the desired ratio of alloy to mercury.

14. Trituration

Trituration (mixing of amalgam is accomplished by the use of an electrically activated mechanical amalgamator or by hand trituration using a glass mortar and pestle.

a. Mechanical Trituration. This method employs a mechanical amalgamator which mixes the amalgam in a capsule by rapid shaking or vibration. It produces more consistently uniform mixes than does the hand trituration because it eliminates most human variables. It is much faster than the hand method, reducing trituration time to a matter of seconds. The operator must avoid setting the machine into action before the proper time is adjusted and must be careful not to over-triturate. It is important to follow the manufacturer's directions for both amalgamator and alloy.

(1) Special capsules are furnished with the mechanical amalgamator for holding the alloy mercury mixture during trituration. Each capsule is fitted with a cap and a small, rod-like pestle. A small funnel is furnished to help in pouring the previously proportioned alloy-mercury mixture into the capsule. When the mixture has been poured into the capsule, the pestle is inserted, its cap fitted in place, and the capsule is placed into the holder on the vibrating arm of the amalgamator. When using the pellet method, first insert the pestle in the capsule, dispense the required mercury, and then dispense the pellets. Usually one pellet is used for a small mix and two pellets for a large mix.

(2) Trituration is accomplished by setting the time according to the manufacturer's instructions for the alloy and for the type of amalgamator used. The time varies according to the size of the mix being manipulated. The average mixing time is 8 to 12 seconds per pellet. When the selected time has elapsed, the automatic timer will stop the machine.

b. Mortar and Pestle Trituration. In this method, trituration of the alloy-mercury mixture is done by hand with a ground glass or metal mortar and pestle the glass mortar has a ground inner surface to match the ground ends of the pestle. Mortar and pestle must mate to insure complete mixing. Each new mortar and pestle should be mated before use. An old mortar and pestle being used by an operator for the first time after prolonged use by another person must be remated to meet the particular angle at which the operator holds the pestle to the mortar. To mate a mortar and pestle, place a small amount of abrasive paste in the mortar and rotate the pestle in it just as in mixing the alloy and mercury. Repeat the procedure as needed until the two surfaces match perfectly. Then wash and dry the mortar and pestle completely before using them for manipulating alloy and mercury.

(1) Hand pressure, speed of mix, and mixing time all affect the properties of amalgam and should be as directed by the manufacturer. The pestle should be hold in a pen grasp rather than in a palm grasp. Speed of trituration is usually expressed in revolutions per minute. The recommended trituration pressure is 2 to 4 pounds per square inch, which is about the same as

the normal weight of the hand with no additional pressure. The pestle is revolved in the mortar at about 180 revolutions per minute.

(2) Properly proportioned and triturated amalgam results in a soft mass in which all alloy particles have been coated with mercury. To be a good mix the completed mix should show these characteristics-

(a) It does not stick to mortar or pestle. Sticking indicates the mortar and pestle were not mated accurately or too much pressure was applied to the pestle.

(b) The amalgam tends to climb the walls of the mortar but readily drops back into the base of the mortar.

(c) It has no particles of undissolved alloy. The presence of particles indicates insufficient mercury or incomplete mix.

(d) It has a silvery, flaky appearance.

15. Mulling the Mix

a. If mulling of the mix is desired after using the mechanical amalgamator, remove the pestle from the capsule and replace the mix in the capsule. Place the capsule back on the machine and vibrate it for 1 to 2 seconds. Or the mix may be mulled by placing it on a cotton squeeze cloth or a piece of rubber dam or into a finger stall to protect the amalgam from contamination by the fingers. Then the amalgam is rubbed or rolled for a few seconds to produce the consistency desired by the dental officer.

b. If mulling is desired after using the mortar and pestle method, empty the mix directly from the mortar onto a cotton squeeze cloth. Fold the squeeze cloth about the amalgam and rub or roll it as in an above. The rubber dam or finger stall also may be used.

16. Elimination of Free Mercury

a. After trituration and mulling, the amalgam mix will contain free mercury which must be expressed by squeezing. To do this, the mix is placed on a squeeze cloth, which is folded over the mix. Then the squeeze cloth is twisted with finger pressure, forcing free mercury out of the amalgam. The dentist will tell the dental assistant how much mercury to express. Depending upon the requirements of insertion, he may have the assistant express a slight amount of mercury or none and then, about halfway through the insertion, have all the free mercury expressed in a single action before continuing insertion of the amalgam into the cavity preparation. After the free mercury has been expressed, the mix is ready for insertion into the cavity preparation. The squeeze cloth is opened and the amalgam carrier loaded by forcing the open cylinder of the amalgam carrier into the balled amalgam.

b. Some dentist divides the mulled amalgams into segments before or after squeezing. If the mix is divided before squeezing, each segment then is squeezed just before it is used.

17. Special Precautions in Preparing Amalgam

a. Any portion of amalgam which is too dry or has begun to crystallize must be discarded. Its use would result in a weak, nonhomogeneous mass. For large restorations it may be necessary to prepare two or more mixes, preparing each mix as needed.

b. Amalgam should be mixed carefully. Free mercury in the restoration will cause excessive expansion and flow and decrease crushing strength. Over trituration by any method will result in decreased expansion or contraction and shorter setting time. Conversely, under trituration will result in excessive expansion and lengthened setting time. Mercury must never be added after mixing has started.

c. Contamination of the amalgam by moisture must be avoided.

Section III. DENTAL CEMENTS

18. General

Dental cements are generally low strength materials prepared by mixing a powder with a liquid. These cements vary in chemical composition, properties, and uses. They are more natural in appearance, are easy to manipulate, and have lower heat conductivity than metallic restorative materials. Dental cements, however, have the disadvantages of a relatively low crushing strength, varying degrees of solubility in mouth fluids, and setting shrinkage. Although used extensively in restorative dentistry, dental cements are among the least permanent restorative materials. Three types of cement are commonly used in dentistry: zinc phosphate cement, silicate cement, and zinc oxide and eugenol cement.

19. Zinc Phosphate Cement

a. *General.* Zinc phosphate cement is a nonpermanent material which may be used to restore teeth in any part of the mouth but is used most often for cementing crowns, fixed partial dentures (bridges), inlays, and certain dental appliances into place. It is also used widely for temporary restorations and intermediate bases. It is made in different shades to match tooth color beneath a translucent restoration. Zinc phosphate cement is supplied as powder and liquid which are mixed to obtain the desired product.

b. *Chemical Composition.*

(1) The composition of zinc phosphate cement powder varies from manufacturer to manufacturer but usually contains between 75 and 100 percent zinc oxide. The powder may also contain modifiers such as silica dioxide, magnesium oxide, copper silicate, bismuth trioxide, and pigments to alter its color.

(2) The liquid used with this powder is phosphoric acid and water in the ratio of about two parts acid to one part water. The solution contains aluminum hydroxide and often zinc oxide. Water content is critical. Water gain hastens setting time. Water loss lengthens setting time. The water content of the liquid is adjusted by the manufacturer to provide satisfactory setting. Care must be taken to preserve this established balance in water content. Liquids exposed in open bottles or on mixing slabs absorb moisture from the air if humidity is high and lose moisture if humidity is low. The liquid bottle should be kept tightly stoppered except when liquid is being withdrawn. Liquid which has been left unstoppered for a long period, is discolored, or is the last 25 percent in the bottle should be discarded.

(3). The manufacture of zinc phosphate cement is carefully controlled. Although cements made by different manufacturers are similar, satisfactory results cannot be attained by mixing the powder of one brand of cement with the liquid of another brand.

c. Properties.

(1) The advantages of zinc phosphate cement are its inconspicuous appearance, speed and ease of manipulation, and enough flow to form a very thin layer for the cementing of closely adapted crowns, fixed partial dentures, and inlays. One reason for using zinc phosphate beneath a metallic restoration is that its low thermal conductivity makes it an excellent insulator. This protects the pulp from sudden temperature changes transmitted by the permanent restoration.

(2) One disadvantage of zinc phosphate cement is its low crushing strength, which varies between 12,000 and 19,000 pounds per square inch. Another disadvantage is that it is slightly soluble in mouth fluids. In time, a zinc phosphate cement restoration would be washed from the cavity preparation. Its setting shrinkage also limits the use of the cement as a restorative material. Due to its opacity, zinc phosphate cement is not a lifelike restorative material on visible surfaces.

(3) The strength of phosphate cements can be increased to a certain point by increasing the ratio of powder to liquid in the mix. For this reason, the dental specialist should use as thick a mix as is practical for the work being performed. Although most of the acidity of phosphate is dissipated after several hours of setting, freshly mixed cement is extremely acid and the thinner the mix is the greater is its early acidity. This acidity sometimes irritates dental pulps when placed next to them. Thick mixes minimize this problem.

d. Setting Reactions. The chemical reaction between the powder and liquid of setting phosphate cement produces heat. The amount of heat produced depends upon the rate of reaction, the size of the mix, and the amount of heat extracted by the mixing slab. The setting time of zinc phosphate cement is normally between 4 and 10 minutes. The manipulative factors used to maintain and prolong the normal setting time are lowering the temperature of the mixing slab between 65° and 75°F (if the slab is not cooled below the temperature at which moisture will condense on it), slow incorporation of the powder, mixing over a large area of the cool slab, and, within optimum limits, using a longer mixing time. The less powder used in ratio to the liquid the longer the cement will take to harden. Good technique minimizes the rise in temperature and acidity of the setting cement which can injure the pulp. The setting reaction consists of dissolving the surface of powder particles by the liquid, resulting in a supersaturated solution which crystallizes and encases the undisclosed powder particle. This condition is typical of a cored structure found in most dental materials of this type. The undisclosed powder particles are called the core, and the crystalline phase encasing them is called the matrix. Generally, for increased strength, decreased shrinkage, and resistance to solubility, it is advisable to incorporate as much powder as possible to reach desired consistencies.

e. Clinical Uses. Zinc phosphate is used as an intermediate base, a cementing medium, and a temporary restoration.

(1) A thick mix of zinc phosphate cement is used as an intermediate base beneath a permanent restoration. The layer of phosphate cement used as a base under metallic restorations protects the pulp from thermal shock. When used under silicate cement restorations, the cement protects the pulp from irritation by the acid of the silicate.

(2) Zinc phosphate cement is used to cement crowns, inlays, and fixed partial dentures permanently into place upon remaining tooth structure. It is also used to hold splints, orthodontic appliances, and other appliances in place upon teeth, to cement facings to bridges, and to cement certain types of artificial teeth to artificial denture bases. A thin mix of cement is used to seat the restoration or appliance completely into place. The cementing medium does not cement two objects together as ordinary glue does. Instead the cement holds the objects

together by mechanical interlocking, filling the space between the irregularities of the tooth preparation and the cemented restoration.

(3) A thick mix of phosphate cement is often used as a temporary restorative material when restorative work cannot be completed at one appointment or when it is inadvisable or impractical to insert a more lasting restorative material. Silver alloy filings are sometimes included in the mix to make the material more resistant to wear if it is to be left in place a long time.

f. Equipment for Manipulation.

g. Proportioning Powder and Liquid. Although desirable, a measuring device is not usually employed for proportioning the powder. The amount of each ingredient will depend on the amount desired and the operation to be performed. Experience gained in manipulation and desired consistencies will enable the dental assistant to estimate accurately the amount of powder to be used according to the number of drops of liquid dispensed. The closely estimated powder is placed on one end of the cool, dry glass slab and divided into six equal segments. An additional small amount of powder is often placed on the corner of the glass slab for use if the estimated powder is insufficient for the desired mix. The liquid is dispensed with the dropper supplied by the manufacturer. Usually 3 drops of liquid are used for a thick mix and, depending on the dentist's needs, 4 or more for the thin mix. The drops are dispensed in the center of the slab or they may be dispensed over a wide area. The close estimation of powder, according to type of mix and number of drops, and the small increments will enhance the slow incorporation of powder which slows the setting reaction, enabling the manipulator to incorporate the maximum amount of powder to attain desired consistencies. This will help obtain cement with optimum physical properties.

h. Mixing. Mixing is done by the slow incorporation of the segments one at a time. This procedure aids in neutralizing the acid and achieving a smooth consistency. A considerable portion of the slab is used. Mixing is done with a moderate circular motion of the spatula blade held flat against the slab. The spatula should be rotated occasionally to incorporate the material that collects on the top of the blade. A good rule is to spatulate for about 20 seconds before adding the next segment. If this is done the mixing time is not critical and completion of the mix will take about 1 1/2 minutes. It is important to reach the desired consistency by using more powder and not to allow a thinner mix to stiffen by crystallization.

i. Characteristics of Completed Mixes. When a thick mix is ready for use it will have a puttylike consistency and a dull, glossless appearance. When a thin mix is ready for use, it will be similar in appearance to thick cream. When material for a thin mix is freshly mixed, if a drop on the end of the spatula is placed on the slab and the spatula is raised, the material left on the slab will peak, hold its form momentarily and gradually spread out.

j. Precautions.

(1) Prevent loss or gain of moisture in liquid cement by keeping bottles tightly stoppered.
(2) Dispense drops only when ready to mix.
(3) Use a cool, dry slab which has not been cooled below the dew point.
(4) Use the same brand of powder and liquid.
(5) Add increments of powder slowly.
(6) Use the maximum amount of powder to obtain the desired consistency. To incorporate the most powder, mix the material in a moderate circular motion over a large area of the slab, turning the spatula often.

20. Copper Phosphate Cements

Two types of phosphate cements containing copper oxides have been used in dentistry. They are the red and black copper cements which derive their color from the presence of red cuprous oxide or black cupric oxide. Basically, the copper cements are zinc phosphate cements with copper salts added to the powder, although occasionally the powder may contain 100 percent cupric oxide. The addition of copper is said to produce cement with a germicidal action in the mouth, but this is doubted by many authorities. Although some cement probably is germicidal when first mixed because of the acid in the liquid, this germicidal factor does not persist for any length of time. Many operators use the copper cements in the posterior deciduous teeth when proper preparation has been difficult because of the age of the patient. Their use is diminishing due to high pulpal toxicity and the doubt cast on the germicidal action.

21. Silicate Cements

a. General. Silicate cement is a nonmetallic, permanent-type restorative material used to restore nonstressbearing parts of carious anterior teeth and other teeth where esthetics (appearance) is important. This is because silicate cement, sometimes incorrectly called synthetic porcelain, appears translucent and may be mixed to produce a variety of shades to match tooth color. Because of its lifelike appearance, silicate cement is one of the most popular dental cements. It is the least permanent of the so-called permanent restorative materials.

b. Instruments and Materials Setup.

c. Chemical Composition.

(1) Silicate cement powder is a complex material made of finely ground ceramic compositions which are essentially acid soluble glasses. Its makeup varies with the manufacturer. The main constituent is silica. Other major ingredients are alumina, lime, and fluoride fluxes. Since the color of silicate cement powder can readily be affected by contamination with dust and dirt, the powder must be protected all the time and the mixing instruments thoroughly clean. A single part of soot to 100,000 parts of powder will cause a detectable change in color.

(2) Silicate cement liquid is similar to the liquid zinc phosphate cement liquid. Both are solutions of phosphoric acid which are partly neutralized by zinc oxide and alumina.

(3) The water content of silicate liquid is carefully established by the manufacturer because it is a critical factor in determining the rate and nature of the setting reaction of mixed silicate cement. The liquid consists of about six parts of phosphoric acid to one part of water. Too little water in the liquid increases setting time. An excess of water decreases setting time.

(4) Bottles containing silicate cement liquid should be kept tightly stoppered when not in use to avoid gain or loss of moisture by exposure to the air. To minimize effects of changes in water content of the liquid, manufacturers supply one-third to one-half more liquid than is needed to mix one bottle of silicate powder. Therefore, when 75 percent of the liquid in any bottle has been used, the remaining portion should be discarded.

(5) Liquid designed for silicate cement should not be mixed with zinc phosphate cement, and phosphate cement liquid should not be mixed with silicate cement. Powders and liquids of different brands are not interchangeable and are not to be mixed.

d. Properties.

(1) The major advantage of silicate cement over metallic restorative materials is its natural appearance. It can be prepared to match very closely the shade of the tooth being restored. Its translucency is similar to that of natural tooth structure. Other advantages are its relative ease and speed of manipulation and low conductivity of heat. Another advantage of silicates is that their thermal dimensional change is almost the same as that of tooth structure. Thus, despite the amount of thermal change, tooth structure and silicate will vary in dimension at about the same rate.

(2) Properties that limit the use of silicate cement are low crushing and edge strength, brittleness, setting contraction, some solubility in mouth fluids, and a comparatively short life expectancy.

(a) The crushing strength of silicate cement is between 23,000 and 24,000 psi. In comparison, the crushing strength of enamel is 100,000 psi, amalgam 45,000 psi, and dentin 30,000 psi.

(b) Silicate cement is more brittle than metals and alloys. This makes the cement unsatisfactory when used on occlusal and incisal surfaces, which is why the dental officer does not bevel the margins of cavities prepared for insertion of silicate cement. Brittleness must always be considered in evaluating a dental restorative material.

(c) Silicate will shrink slightly upon setting. This results in staining around margins. If insufficient powder is added to the mix the degree of shrinkage is much greater.

(d) Silicate cement is soluble in the fluids of the mouth. Excess liquid in the mix increases the solubility of the cement. For this reason, the liquid should be thoroughly incorporated with as much powder as can be wetted. Because of this solubility, it is often necessary to replace "washed out" silicate restorations.

e. Setting Reactions. The setting reaction of silicate cement is one in which the outer surface of powder particles is dissolved in the liquid to form silicic acid and phosphates. The silicic acid molecules unite to form a rigid gel. The final result is an interlocked mixture of phosphate crystals, undisclosed particles of powder, and hardened silica gel. The reaction starts rapidly but gradually slows. The temperature has a decided effect on the rate of reaction which in turn determines the amount of powder that can be incorporated in the mix. The silica gel must not be disturbed while forming. Once broken, the parts will not rejoin. Silicate cement that is worked while it is setting becomes. a crumbly or powdery mass.

f. Proportioning Powder and Liquid. When preparing silicate cement, use a glass slab which is reserved only for the mixing of silicate cements and a plastic spatula. The slab should be marked on one end with an "S" to show it is for use only with silicate. It should be clean and free of nicks, scratches, and breaks. Slabs never should be interchanged. Steel spatulas should not be used because they are affected by acid in the silicate liquid and they will contaminate the mix. Before the materials are measured out, the glass slab should be cooled by being placed in water at 65° to 75°F. This should be followed by thorough drying of slab and spatula.

(1) The first step in preparing the cement is to place the portion of powder near the center of the slab. The dentist may have selected a shade which requires blending of powder from two or more bottles. The proper proportion of each should be placed on the slab. An additional small amount of powder should be placed in the corner of the slab to serve as a reserve. With experience, the dental specialist can closely estimate the proper amount of powder to place on the slab. The powder is then divided in halves, and one half is divided into thirds.

(2) Next, place two or three drops of liquid near the powder on the slab. Hold the dropper in a vertical position so that the drops will be uniform in size and let the drops form slowly before falling onto the slab.

g. *Mixing Silicate Cement.* Starting with the large segment, the powder is incorporated in the liquid one segment at a time, using the spatula in a rapid folding manner and using light pressure. Each segment is mixed only until wet throughout and the next segment is then immediately added. Since the gel structure is almost completely formed after 1 minute, the total mixing time should not exceed 60 seconds. The normal setting time of silicate cement is between 3 and 8 minutes. The only safe way to maintain and prolong the setting reaction is to lower the temperature of the mixing slab. Slabs are usually cooled between 65° and 76°F for mixing if this is not below the point where moisture condenses on the slab. To avoid disturbing the gel, the mix must be completed in 1 minute so the reaction will occur when the material is confined and conformed in the cavity preparation.

h. *Characteristics of a Completed Mix.* When the mix is ready for use, it will have a heavy dough-like appearance and consistency. A glossy appearance or stickiness indicates too little powder. Flakiness indicates too much powder or prolonged mixing. Optimum properties are attained only by using the maximum of powder within the limitation that all powder particles are wetted by the liquid and mixing time is not exceeded. Too little or too much powder or prolonged mixing time will lower the physical properties previously discussed.

i. *Precautions.*

(1) Preserve acid-water ratio.

    (a) Keep bottles tightly stoppered.
    (b) Discard bottles of liquid when 25 percent remains or if they have been left open.

    (c) Use dry equipment which has not been cooled below the dew point.
    (d) Dispense drops only when ready to mix.
    (e) Use the same brand of powder and liquid.

(2) To maintain the desired shade, you must use clean equipment and clean technique.

(3) Use a slab which is properly cooled and free of nicks and scratches.

(4) Mix rapidly within the limitation of mixing time.

(5) Use the maximum powder to get the desired consistency.

22. Zinc Oxide and Eugenol Cement

This cement, composed of a powder that is basically zinc oxide and a liquid known as eugenol, is used for many dental purposes ranging from temporary restorative materials to surgical dressings and impression pastes.

    a. Chemical Composition. Zinc oxide is dispensed as a powder, eugenol as a liquid. They are mixed together the same way as zinc phosphate cement. By National Bureau of Standards specifications, the powder must contain between 70 and 100 percent zinc oxide. The manufacturer may add hydrogenated resins to increase strength and zinc acetate to hasten the set. Eugenol is usually derived from oil of cloves because it contains more eugenol (82 percent) than do the oils of cinnamon, orange, or bay. Eugenol is an obtundent (pain-relieving agent). It is a clear liquid which gradually changes to amber when exposed to light.

    b. Physical Properties. This cement soothes pain, makes tissue less sensitive to pain, is slightly antiseptic, and is low in thermal conductivity. It is protective because it provides a good marginal seal when placed in tooth cavities. The crushing strength of pure zinc oxide and eugenol cement is about 2,000 psi, which is low in comparison to that of other cements. The crushing strength can be increased to 5,000 psi by the addition of hydrogenated resin.

    c. Uses.

    (1) The most frequent use of zinc oxide-eugenol cement is as a treatment restoration. When placed for treatment of fractured teeth, lost restorations, advanced caries, and pulpitis it helps prevent pulpal irritation and exerts a palliative effect on the pulp.

    (2) It is used as a temporary cementing medium for crowns; inlays, and fixed partial dentures that may later be cemented more permanently with zinc phosphate cement.

    (3) It is used as an intermediate base to provide insulation between metallic restorations and vital tooth structure. Because of the cement's low crushing strength, its use for this purpose is sometimes contraindicated where the base is expected to support a permanent restoration. Usually, when the base is to support a permanent restoration, the dentist will require a zinc phosphate cement base to place over the zinc oxide and eugenol cement.

    (4) It is used in pulp capping for near and direct exposures of the pulp but this use is declining. Calcium hydroxide is usually used for pulp capping.

    (5) It is used as a surgical packing or dressing after certain oral surgery procedures. An example of this is the surgical dressing applied and adapted over the gingival area after a gingivectomy. This dressing protects the area and makes the tissue less sensitive.

Section IV. DENTAL WAXES

23. General

Many different waxes are used in dentistry. The composition, form, and color of each wax are designed to facilitate its use and to produce the best possible results. The discussion in this section is limited to clinical aspects.

24. Inlay Wax

Inlay wax is used to prepare patterns which are to be reproduced in gold or some other material in the fabrication of inlays, crowns, and fixed and removable partial dentures.

a. For success in these procedures, the wax must have properties which enable very close adaptation to the prepared portions of the tooth to be restored; must provide freedom from distortion; must permit detailed carving without flaking or chipping; and must not leave excessive residue when it is removed from a mold by burning. The wax should harden at body temperature but soften at a temperature low enough to permit it to be manipulated in a plastic state in the mouth without injury to pulp or oral tissues. Its color should contrast with the colors of teeth and oral tissues to facilitate carving, except that ivory wax is used to avoid risk of color contamination when porcelain or acrylic resin restorations are constructed. Because of the importance of certain qualities of these waxes, the American Dental Association has developed certain specifications with which an inlay wax must comply to be acceptable.

b. Inlay wax is available in blue, green, ivory or deep purple sticks, preformed shapes for partial dentures, and solidly packed cans. Inlay wax is hard at room temperatures and breaks if bent sharply. This wax remains hard at mouth temperature and may be carved either in or out of the mouth. It is softened with dry heat until plastic or by immersion in warm water.

25. Baseplate Wax

Baseplate wax is used mainly for making occlusion rims and for holding artificial teeth to baseplates during the fabrication of dentures.

a. The wax is composed mainly of beeswax, paraffin, and coloring matter, which is mixed together, cast into blocks, and rolled into sheets. The sheets are red or pink, 3 inches wide and 6 inches long. Baseplate wax is relatively hard and slightly brittle at room temperature but becomes soft and pliable when heated.

b. Baseplate wax must be capable of holding porcelain or acrylic teeth in position at normal room temperature but it should not be brittle. It should maintain uniform consistency at room temperature and at mouth temperature.

c. Two types of baseplate wax, hard and medium, are listed in the Federal supply catalog. The hard type is suitable for use in warm climates but tends to crack and flake at low temperatures. The medium type is suitable for use at low temperatures but flows excessively at high temperatures.

26. Sticky Wax

Sticky wax becomes sticky when melted and has the property of adhering to the surfaces of various materials. Sticky wax is composed of beeswax, paraffin, and resins. It is usually supplied as hexagonal sticks of various colors, often orange or purple. It is brittle at room temperature and assumes a thick liquid consistency when heated. The wax has many uses in a dental clinic or laboratory. For example, it is used to hold together broken pieces of a denture being repaired and to assemble and hold together components of fixed partial dentures and wrought partial dentures in preparation for soldering.

27. Utility Wax

Utility wax is a pliable wax issued in stick form. Its most common uses are: providing rim locks and otherwise adapting impression trays for individual impressions, building up post-dam areas on impressions, and forming a bead or border on preliminary and final impressions. Utility wax is plastic and tacky at room temperature and so it may be used without heating. It is usually red in color.

28. Disclosing Wax

Disclosing wax is used to determine points of unequal pressure in a denture. These points, which may be causing discomfort to the patient, are located by painting the wax on the tissue side of the denture base and holding the denture in place under pressure in the mouth. The wax flows away from the pressure points, revealing the points needing relief.

29. Boxing Wax

Boxing wax is used to form a box around impressions of the mouth when making a cast (model). This boxing limits the flow of gypsum material, either plaster or stone. Boxing wax is usually issued in red strips, measuring about 1 1/2 inches wide, 12 inches long, and 1/8 inch thick. The wax is soft and pliable at room temperature, making it easy to form. For further softening a strip of wax can be passed through an open flame.

30. Impression Wax

Impression wax is discussed with impression materials in paragraph 44.

Section V. GOLD AND GOLD ALLOYS

31. General

For most dental purposes, pure gold cannot be used alone because it is too soft; however, it can be combined with other metals to produce alloys which can be used to fabricate every type of dental restoration or prosthesis where metal is indicated. The basic types of gold alloys used in dentistry are casting gold, gold solder, wrought gold, and gold plate. The principal metals used to combine with gold for dental gold alloys are silver, copper, platinum, palladium, and zinc. The following discussion of dental gold and gold alloys is limited to aspects of clinical interest.

32. Fineness, Carat, and Weighing

The amount of gold in a gold alloy may be rated in terms of fineness or carat. Fineness is determined by the parts per thousand of pure gold contained in the alloy. In terms of fineness, pure gold is 1,000 fine, and an alloy with three-fourths pure gold is 750 fine. In the carat system of rating, the carat refers to the parts of gold determined by dividing the substance into 24 units and then counting the number of units of gold. Thus, a 24-carat substance would be pure gold and a 12-carat alloy would be one-half gold. In weighing precious metals like gold and platinum the troy system of weight is used. In this system, the basic units of measurement of alloy quantity are grains, pennyweights, and ounces. Gold alloys are recorded and issued by the troy system as indicated below.

24 grains (grs)	=1 pennyweight (dwt)
20 pennyweights (dwt)	=1 ounce (oz)
12 ounces (oz)	= 1 pound (lb)

33. Casting Gold Alloy

Casting gold alloy is used in the fabrication of various restorations. It is alloyed and made into ingots suitable for melting and casting into molds for the restorations. Casting gold alloy may be classed into four types: soft, which is used for inlays not subjected to stress; medium, which is used for ordinary inlay work; hard, which is used for full crowns, three-quarter crowns, and retainers; and extra hard, which is used for saddles, clasps, and one-piece cast partial dentures. Alloyed casting gold can be whitened (white gold) by adding palladium, platinum, or silver and used for crowns and abutments requiring great strength and hardness.

34. Annealing and Tempering Gold Alloys

Through the use of controlled heat and rate of cooling, gold alloys can be annealed (softened) or tempered (hardened). Gold alloys are hardened by slow cooling. This is the opposite of steel which is softened by slow cooling. Rapid cooling from a high temperature will soften a gold alloy but harden steel. Rapid cooling is done by quenching the heated gold alloy in tap water.

35. Gold Alloy Solder

Gold alloy solder is used for joining the parts of fixed partial dentures, for building up or forming restorations, and for gold repairs. Soldering is the process of joining metals by means of a solder or a lower fusing metal.

36. Wrought Gold Alloy

Wrought gold alloy is used in dentistry for the construction of clasps and orthodontic appliances.

37. Gold Foil

Gold foil is a restorative material in which the metal is used in a pure state. It is an excellent material for permanently restoring tooth structure and is used most often for restorations on facial surfaces, proximal surfaces on anterior teeth. and occlusal surfaces of posterior teeth Its chief disadvantages are color high thermal conductivity, and difficulty in manipulation. Gold foil is available in either an adhesive or a nonadhesive form. To prevent pellets of adhesive foil from sticking together before use, their surfaces are treated with moisture or gas residues. When ready for use, the moisture and gas residues are vaporized by heating.

38. Gold Plate

Gold plate is used less often than are casting gold alloys, wrought gold alloy, or gold alloy solder. It is used in the fabrication of some types of crowns and often used in repair procedures, such as repairing a hole in a gold crown with solder.

Section VI. DENTAL IMPRESSION MATERIALS

39. General

a. An essential preliminary step in constructing prosthetic restorations is obtaining an accurate cast (model) of the patient's mouth (maxillary or mandibular arch or both). This is done by making an impression, which is a mold or negative reproduction, of the teeth and their surrounding tissues or of edentulous (without teeth) areas, using one of the impression materials described below. The cast then is formed by pouring artificial stone or other suitable material in the mold.

b. One method of classifying impression materials is the way in which they harden. Plaster of paris and metallic oxide impression pastes, for instance, harden by chemical action. Modeling plastic (impression compound), however, softens when heated and hardens when cooled, without a chemical change. These materials which soften under heat and solidify when cooled, without chemical change, are classed as thermoplastic substances.

c. Impression materials also may be classified according to rigidity, plasticity, elasticity, and use. Perhaps the better way to classify them is according to their rigidity when set. Impression materials that are inelastic when set include modeling plastic, impression plaster, and metallic oxide impression paste. Elastic impression materials include the hydrocolloids and polysulfide and silicone base impression materials. The uses, properties, and manipulation of these materials are discussed below. The manufacturers' instructions should be followed in all cases. Variables in specific information stated below apply in most cases.

d. A good impression material has the following desirable qualities:

(1) It is plastic at a temperature which is comfortable to the patient.

(2) It does not irritate the mouth.

(3) It sets completely at or slightly above mouth temperature.

(4) It sets uniformly and without distortion during setting.

(5) It is cohesive but not adhesive.

(6) After it solidifies, the material does not flake when trimmed with a sharp knife at room temperature.

(7) It does not change shape or dimensions at normal room temperature and humidity.

40. Modeling Plastic Materials

a. Modeling plastic materials, which are moldable thermoplastic substances, are used extensively to make impressions for complete dentures, inlays, and fixed partial dentures. They are used alone or with other impression materials to form trays and for post-seal and border molding of impressions. These materials become grainy and brittle with insufficient heat, and sticky and adhesive with excessive heat.

b. Modeling plastic materials are supplied in colors indicative of their softening or working temperatures. The types most often used are cake form (red cake and black cake) and stick form (red stick and green stick). Black cake is harder and softens at a higher temperature than red cake. For this reason it is considered more a tray material and less a true impression material than the red cake. Green stick type is a low-heat material used for impressions for crowns, fixed partial dentures, post-dam (seal at the posterior border of maxillary edentulous impressions), and establishing peripheral borders of edentulous impressions.

c. A typical formula for modeling plastic material is 45 percent shellac, 30 percent talc, 2.5 percent glycerin, and 22.5 percent wax, palm oil, tallow, and coloring matter.

d. Red cake modeling plastic softens in a water bath between 130° and 140°F. Black modeling plastic material must be heated between 140° and 150°F before its working temperature is reached. Green modeling plastic material softens between 120° and 130°F. In each case, the manufacturer prescribes the correct temperature of the water. The water must cover the material completely to assure uniform softening. Gauze is placed over the tray in the water bath to keep the modeling plastic material from sticking to the metal. This also facilitates cleaning the water bath later. Red and green stick types have the same compositions and working temperatures as the corresponding cakes.

e. When soft and smooth, the modeling plastic material is adapted to the tray previously selected by the dental officer. For complete maxillary edentulous impressions, the material is rolled into a ball and pressed down into the tray as desired. For complete mandibular impressions, the material is rolled into a cylinder-shaped mass for insertion into the tray. After it is adapted to the tray, the material is brushed with a flame to remove fissures and fingerprints. All that remains to be done before making the impression is the tempering (moistening and returning to proper temperature) of the material by dipping the tray containing the material momentarily into the water bath.

41. Metallic Oxide Impression Paste

a. General. Metallic oxide impression paste is used as a corrective impression material in denture fabrication. It is also used to make impressions for rebasing or relining dentures. Metallic oxide impression paste is usually supplied in separate tubes as a base and a hardener, which are mixed together. When mixed, the ingredients will harden in the mouth, allowing enough time for the molding of the border of the impression by the dentist to accommodate muscle attachments. The base ingredient usually is zinc oxide, which is premixed with inert oil (linseed) to form one of the pastes. The liquid or hardener ingredient (eugenol) is premixed with inert powder to form the other paste. The two constituents of metallic oxide impression paste (base and hardener) are usually of different colors.

b. Manipulation. The two pastes are usually mixed on a parchment pad with a stainless steel spatula or a tongue blade. The correct proportion is obtained by squeezing equal lengths of material from the tubes onto the mixing pad. Both sides of the spatula are wiped in the brown paste. Then the brown paste is mixed into the pink paste and is spatulated until a uniform color without streaks is obtained. Mixing time is generally 1 minute. Before the selected tray is loaded, the mix should be spread over the mixing area to express any air bubbles. Then the entire mix is picked up and the tray is loaded. If the material sets too rapidly a drop of oleic acid or petrolatum may be added during mixing to retard the set. If it sets too slowly, a drop of water is added. Before mixing the paste, the dental assistant should spread petrolatum around the lips, cheeks, and chin of the patient to prevent the paste from sticking to the patient's face.

42. Hydrocolloids

a. General. Hydrocolloids are elastic impression materials with which accurate impressions of oral tissues, including undercuts and other interferences, can be obtained readily and accurately. An undercut (fig. 9) is a hard or soft tissue area so located that it mechanically resists or prevents insertion or removal of restorations, impressions, or other material. Hydrocolloids are used for making impressions for fabricating complete dentures, fixed and removable partial dentures, crowns, and inlays and for duplicating casts. Hydrocolloid materials will deform momentarily, thus allowing the impression to be withdrawn, but will regain its original shape which accurately reproduces tissues as they exist in the oral cavity.

b. Types. The two basic types of hydrocolloids are reversible (agar), which can be softened by heat and hardened by cooling and can be used repeatedly, and irreversible (alginate), which hardens when mixed with water and cannot be softened again. Irreversible hydrocolloid is obtained in a large can or a small individual pack. The manufacturer's mixing instructions are always followed. Both materials are composed mostly of water. After the impression is made, the gel consists of fibrils of gelled material suspended in water. If water is lost by evaporation or synerisis (exudation of water from inside the material) the impression will shrink. If the hydrocolloid is placed in water, it is subject to imbibitions (uptake of water) and it will swell. There is no effective way to store the hydrocolloid impression, and the cast must be poured at once.

c. Manipulation.

(1) Reversible (agar) hydrocolloid. Special conditioners are used for manipulating reversible hydrocolloid. Various types are available with a compartment for boiling, storing, and conditioning the material. Syringes are used to inject the material onto critical areas and a water-cooled tray is used for gelation of the impression. The first step is to reduce the hydrocolloid gel to a fluid sol by placing the filled syringes and tubes in boiling water for 10 minutes. If a material is reliquefied after a previous gelling, at least 3 minutes should be added to the boiling time, since each time this material is reduced to a sol and the gel allowed to reform, it is harder to break down. Insufficient boiling results in a grainy, stiff mass that will not produce the fine detail required. After the material is liquefied, it may be stored in the storage compartment until needed. A storage bath temperature of 150°F is usually ideal. A lower temperature may result in partial gelation and inaccurate reproduction of fine detail. Before the dentist can make the impression, the material must be cooled or tempered in the conditioning bath. This conditioning will increase the viscosity of the material so it will not flow out of the tray or cause discomfort to the patient. The hydrocolloid is expressed from the tube into the preselected tray and placed in the conditioning bath for 10 minutes at 115°F. Then the dental assistant passes the filled syringe to the dentist. While the dentist is covering the critical areas in the mouth, the assistant should remove the tray from the bath and scrape the water-soaked outer layer from the material in the tray. This step is necessary for a complete bonding between the hydrocolloid in the tray and the injected hydrocolloid. The tray is passed to the dentist who makes the impression. Gelation of the hydrocolloid is accomplished by the circulation through the tray of cool water (60° to 70°F) for at least 5 minutes.

(2) Irreversible (alginate) hydrocolloid. Special equipment is not required to manipulate irreversible hydrocolloid but the manufacturer's directions for mixing it must be followed strictly. Directions for the temperature of the water, proportions of powder to water, and mixing time are most important in preserving the gel strength. Maximum gel strength is required to prevent fracture and assure elastic recovery. Mixing time is especially important; 1 minute is usually specified. Too little spatulation may reduce gel strength as much as 50 percent. Too much spatulation will break the gel as it forms and reduce gel strength. The required measurement of powder is sifted into the measured amount of water in a rubber mixing bowl to minimize the trapping of air bubbles. The mix is stirred vigorously for the specified time, monitored by a time clock. Then the dental specialist loads the material in a preselected tray in such a way as to avoid trapping air bubbles. Excess material in the bowl is usually given to the dentist to cover certain areas in the mouth. Then the dental specialist passes the filled tray to the dentist who makes the impression.

43. Polysulfide Base Impression Material

a. General.

(1) This material is used to make impressions for crowns, inlays, fixed and removable partial dentures, and complete dentures, especially in areas containing undercuts. It is composed of synthetic polysulfide base material and accelerator. It is supplied as pastes which, when mixed properly, solidify to an elastic condition. The material comes in two tubes, one tube

containing polysulfide base material (white paste), and the other containing accelerator (brown paste).

(2) Several polysulfide base impression materials are available. Most of them can be obtained in light (injectible), heavy, and regular types. The light type is used with the heavy type for gold restorations and removable partial dentures. The regular type is used mostly for complete dentures.

b. Manipulation.

(1) When using polysulfide base impression material, the dental specialist will need the following items: a customized tray, a syringe, light and medium or heavy-bodied polysulfide base impression material, and an adhesive. The customized tray is usually made of acrylic resin and constructed on a cast obtained from a preliminary impression of irreversible hydrocolloid material.

(2) Normally, a multiple mix technique is employed. The tray material (heavy or medium bodied) is mixed first. Equal lengths of the two pastes (brown accelerator and white polysulfide base) are expressed on a parchment pad and spatulated until the color of the mix is uniform without streaks. Then the material is placed in the tray, whose inner surface has been painted with an adhesive, and set aside. Next the syringe material is mixed the same way as the tray material. The syringe is filled and passed to the dentist who injects the material into the prepared area of the mouth. The filled tray then is passed to the dentist.

(3) The work of the dentist and the dental assistant must be timed so that neither the tray nor the syringe material has cured to the extent that they do not bond when brought together. If the material sets too rapidly the set may be retarded by adding a drop of oleic acid during mixing or by cooling the tubes in a refrigerator before mixing. If the material sets too slowly, a drop of water is added to hasten the set.

44. Impression Wax (Iowa Wax)

Impression wax may be used to make corrective linings for complete and partial denture impressions. It may be used also for corrective lining impressions for rebasing dentures. The patient's original denture teeth are used and a new acrylic base is processed.

Section VII. CAST MATERIALS

45. Gypsum Products

A number of gypsum products are used in dentistry. Plaster of paris and artificial stone powder are the ones used most as cast materials.

46. Chemistry of Gypsum Products

A general understanding of the chemistry of gypsum products will enable the dental specialist to use them wisely and increase his knowledge of why they react as they do. Gypsum is composed mainly of calcium sulphate dihydrate. A dihydrate is a material consisting of two parts of water to one part of the compound. Calcium sulphate dihydrate therefore is one part calcium dihydrate and two parts water.

a. In the manufacturing process gypsum is converted to plaster of paris and artificial stone by a process called calcining. Methods of calcining differ for plaster of paris, type I artificial stone, and type II artificial stone (die stone) except that in all processes the gypsum is first ground to a fine powder of particle size. Plaster of paris is derived when the gypsum is subjected to heat in an open vat. Type I artificial stone is produced when the gypsum is processed by steam heat under pressure. Type II artificial stone (die stone) is made by boiling the gypsum in a 30 percent solution of calcium chloride. The chloride then is washed away and the stone is dried and ground to the desired fineness.

b.   Essentially, in all products, the reaction converts calcium sulphate dehydrate in to calcium sulphate hemihydrates by the removal of 1 ½ of the 2 molecules of water ($2C_aSO_4 \cdot 2H_2O$ + heat$\rightarrow$ $(C_aSO_4)_2 \cdot H_2O + 3H_2O$). The properties of the different products are due to the particle size and structure of the resulting powder that determine the amount of water necessary to float the powder during manipulation. Chemically the plaster and artificial stone are identical but the plaster particles are rough, irregular, and porous. The artificial stone particles are prismatic, more regular in size and dense. When the plaster or artificial stone is mixed with water, a hard substance is formed and the process described above is reversed ($3H_2O + (C_aSO_4)_2 \cdot H_2O \rightarrow 2CaSO_4 2 \cdot H_2O + heat$). In the setting reaction, crystals of gypsum will form in clusters after the hemihydrates dissolves in the water. These nuclei of crystallization intermesh and become entangled with one another, giving the set material its strength and rigidity. During manipulation enough water must be added so that the reaction will take place. Additional water is needed to float the powder particles so they can be stirred and poured into the impression to form the cast. The more water that must be used for this purpose the weaker the material will be upon set.

47. Uses and Manipulation of Gypsum Products

a. Plaster of Paris.

(1) *Uses.* Plaster of paris is used for pouring casts, making matrices for prosthodontic restorations, attaching casts to articulators, and general use in the dental laboratory where strength is not important. Its crushing strength is 2,600 psi.

(2) *Manipulation.* Water-powder ratios are used as stated by the manufacturer. Before manipulation, the can containing the material should be agitated to disperse evenly all elements in the powder. A clean, dry, rubber bowl and plaster spatula are used to manipulate the material. First, the water is measured and poured into the rubber bowl. The powder is weighed and sifted into the water to avoid trapping air bubbles. Then the mix is spatulated 30 to 60 seconds with a knifing or stirring motion including all powder from the sides of the bowl. Whipping the mix will trap air and so should be avoided. Before the material is poured, the mix is vibrated to remove any air bubbles unintentionally trapped.

(3) *Setting time.* The initial setting time for plaster of paris is 5 to 10 minutes. The initial set is the stage at which the plaster loses its glossy appearance and is hard enough to hold for carving. The final set for plaster of paris is about 45 minutes and is the stage at which the plaster achieves a dry, hard condition. The setting of plaster of paris can be hastened by using less water, by mixing longer, by using chemical accelerators, or by using warm water (up to 85°F). Reversing these processes or using chemical retarders will lengthen the setting time. The most satisfactory results are obtained by following the manufacturer's directions.

b. Artificial Stone.

(1) *Uses.* Artificial stone is used in making master casts and dies and for general laboratory use when a very hard, strong product is needed. Since artificial stone particles are

nonporous, the finished product is hard and dense. This provides an excellent cast for the fabrication of prosthetic restorations. The crushing strength of artificial stone is 7,500 psi.

(2) *Manipulation.* Artificial stone is mixed much like plaster of paris. The average mixing ratio is 30 cc of water to 100 grams of stone powder. This ratio may vary somewhat with different manufacturers. The required amount of water is placed in a rubber bowl and the stone powder added slowly. All powder should be smoothed below the water before spatulating. Spatulation should be thorough without whipping the mixture; whipping can trap air bubbles which weaken the cast. The bowl should be vibrated during the mixing to make air bubbles rise to the surface. Spatulation should be completed in 30 to 60 seconds; after that the bowl should be vibrated again. The use of mechanical spatulation helps to reduce air bubbles.

(3) *Setting time.* The initial setting time for artificial stone is usually 8 to 10 minutes, the final setting time 25 to 45 minutes depending upon the. type of stone mixed. The surface hardness can be increased by soaking the cast several hours in a solution of borax.

Section VIII. MISCELLANEOUS DENTAL MATERIALS

48. Calcium Hydroxide

Calcium hydroxide is a fine white powder used in operative procedures primarily for pulp capping (protection for an exposed or nearly exposed pulp) since this material accelerates the formation of secondary dentin. Calcium hydroxide is available as powder, paste, and liquid. The powder must be mixed with sterile water or xylocaine to form a paste. The paste and liquids are premixed commercial preparations ready for immediate use. Because of its low crushing strength, calcium hydroxide alone is not used as an intermediate base. When applied, it is usually covered with zinc phosphate cement or a zinc oxide and eugenol cement.

49. Root Canal Filling Materials

These materials are used to fill previously prepared root canals. This treatment is part of root canal or endodontic therapy. Root canal filling materials consist of tapered gutta-percha or silver points in various standard sizes and root canal sealers or cements. Root canal cements often consist of a zinc oxide and eugenol preparation. A good root canal filling material is insoluble in tissue fluids, opaque to (not allowing) the passage of x-rays, reasonably easy to remove, nonirritating to periapical (around the apex or root tip) tissues, nonabsorbent to moisture, and dimensionally stable after insertion into a root canal.

a. *Gutta-Percha.* Gutta-percha is used for a temporary filling (supplied as a stick) and as a root canal filling material supplied as points. Gutta-percha is the refined coagulated milky exudate of trees in the Malay Peninsula. It is pink or gray in color. It softens when heated and is easily molded. When cool, it maintains shape fairly well. Gutta-percha points long have been a root canal filling material of choice because of the material's advantages. It has a high thermal expansion. It does not shrink unless used with solvent. It is radiopaque, conducts heat poorly, and is easy to remove from the root canal. It may be kept sterile in antiseptic solution, is impervious to moisture, and is bacterioostatic (prevents the growth or multiplication of bacteria). Disadvantages of gutta-percha are that it shrieks when used with a solvent and is not always easy to introduce into the root canal.

b. Silver Root Canal Points. The dentist may use silver root canal points in filling the root canal. Silver points have the advantages of gutta-percha but are easier to insert. Sight selection of silver points is easy because they come in the same sizes and tapers as standard root canal broaches and reamers. The main disadvantages of silver points are that they are hard to remove from the root canal and are more expensive than gutta-percha.

50. Temporary Stopping Material

Temporary stopping material is used primarily as a temporary filling material. It usually consists of gutta-percha, waxes, zinc oxide, fatty acids, and possibly powdered feldspar or silex. This material dissolves to some extent in fluids of the mouth. It is easier to handle than gutta-percha but does not wear as well. It can be made plastic by heat or by solution in chloroform or eucalyptol.

51. Cavity Lining Varnish

Cavity lining varnish is used as a seal under otherwise unbased restoration. It is composed of resins dissolved in a volative thinner. Cavity lining varnish is used extensively to seal dentin tubules (small tubes in the dentin that contain dentinal fibers) and thus isolate the pulp of the tooth from the acidity of silicate or zinc phosphate cement and in some cases, to help prevent marginal leakage around restorations. Cavity lining varnish is issued premixed, usually with a bottle of thinner. The bottle of varnish should be kept tightly sealed when not in use. If the varnish gets too thick, thinner should be added to restore its original consistency.

52. Dental Resins for Restorative Dentistry

a. General. Resins are used as restorative and denture base materials. (A denture base is that part of a denture which contacts the soft tissues and supports the artificial teeth.) A synthetic resin, methyl methacrylate (acrylic resin), is the most widely used resin for these purposes. Two forms of this material are used: an auto polymerizing type, which sets or cures to form a satisfactory result at room temperatures, and a heat-polymerizing type, which is processed by application of heat under pressure.

b. Composition. Acrylic resins are made as a liquid and a powder which are mixed when ready for use. The liquid, called monomer, is composed of a derivative of methyl acrylic acid, an inhibitor (usually hydroquinone), and a tertiary amine (usually dimethyl-p-toluidine). The autopolymerizing acrylic monomer includes an accelerator. Monomer vaporizes readily in air with characteristic ether-like odor. It must be kept tightly stoppered to prevent evaporation when not in use. Monomer is readily contaminated by other materials and should not be allowed to contact the rubber bulb of the dropper or be stored in the same compartment with eugenol or other essential oils. For this reason, zinc oxide and eugenol cannot be used as a base for resin restorations. The powder, called polymer, is available in a variety of shades which can be mixed to closely match most teeth. Since contaminants can affect the cure and the color of the material, contamination of both polymer and monomer should be avoided.

c. Uses.

(1) Autopolymerizing acrylic resin is used in operative dentistry as a direct restorative material, in the construction of acrylic resin facings for some full crowns, and in the construction of temporary crowns, fixed partial dentures, and space maintainers. It is used in prosthetic dentistry to repair complete and partial dentures, to fabricate individualized impression trays, to fabricate oral surgical and periodontal splints, and as a baseplate material.

(2) Heat-polymerizing acrylic resin is used in restorative dentistry to fabricate crowns and parts of pontics. It is used in prosthetic dentistry to fabricate bases and saddles for dentures, to fabricate individualized impression trays, to fabricate oral surgical and periodontal splints, to repair dentures, and for other purposes.

d. Manipulation. Manufacturer's directions must be followed strictly.

53. Dental Porcelain

Dental porcelain is manufactured as a powder. When it is heated to a very high temperature in a special oven it fuses into a homogeneous mass. The heating process is called baking. Upon cooling, the mass is hard and dense. The material is made in a variety of shades to match closely most tooth colors. Baked porcelain has a translucency similar to that of dental enamel, so that porcelain crowns, pontics, and inlays of highly pleasing appearance can be made. Ingredients of porcelain include feldspar, kaolin, silica in the form of quartz, materials which act as fluxes to lower the fusion point, metallic oxide and binders. Porcelains are classified into high-, medium-, or low-fusing groups, depending upon the temperature at which fusion takes place.

a. High-fusing porcelains fuse at 2,400°F or over. They are used for the fabrication of full porcelain crowns (jacket crowns).

b. Medium-fusing porcelains fuse between 2,000° and 2,300°F. They are used in the fabrication of inlays, crowns, facings, and pontics. A pontic is the portion of a fixed partial denture which replaces a missing tooth.

c. Low-fusing porcelains fuse between 1,600° and 1,950°F. They are used primarily to correct or modify the contours of previously baked high- or medium fusing porcelain restorations.

54. Baseplate Material

Baseplate materials are used in complete and partial denture fabrication, in making the occlusion-rim foundation, and in the fabrication of impression trays. Baseplates are usually softened over an open flame, then molded over a cast and trimmed. They are composed of shellac resins and wax modifiers.

55. Polishing Materials

a. Tin Oxide. Tin oxide is used to polish teeth and restorations. A fine white powder, it is used in paste with water or glycerin.

b. Pumice. Pumice is used as an abrasive and polishing agent for acrylic resins, amalgams, and gold. It consists mainly of complex silicates of aluminum, potassium, and sodium. Two grades of it are listed in the Federal supply catalog: flour of pumice and coarse pumice.

c. Chalk (Whiting). Chalk is used for polishing acrylic resins and metals. It is composed primarily of calcium carbonate.

d. Tripoli. Tripoli is a polishing agent usually used for gold and other metals. It is made from certain porous rocks.

e. Rouge (Jeweler's). Rouge is used for polishing gold and is composed of iron oxide. It is usually in cake or stick form.

f. Zirconium Silicate. Zirconium silicate is used for cleaning and polishing teeth. It may be mixed with water or stannous fluoride solution for caries prevention treatment. Instructions must be followed exactly to obtain the proper powder-liquid proportions for full effectiveness.

56. Intermediate Restorative Material

Intermediate restorative material consists of a powder, that is 80 percent zinc oxide and 20 percent polymethyl methacrylate, which is mixed with a liquid containing 99 percent eugenol and 1 percent acetic acid. Although this a temporary restorative material, its compressive strength is twice that of zinc oxide and eugenol cement and only slightly less than zinc phosphate cement. Its tensile and sheer strengths are greater than zinc phosphate cement. Supplied in three colors, the material is used as follows. Ivory is used in anterior teeth where affected dentin is left in the cavity preparation. Red or pink is used in posterior teeth where affected dentin is left in depth of the cavity preparation. Blue is used in posterior teeth where both affected and infected dentin are removed.

———

GLOSSARY

BASIC DENTAL TERMS

The dental assistant should make every effort to use correct medical and dental terminology. Following is a glossary that defines some of the terms that the dental assistant should know.

Abrasion: The wearing away of tooth structure as a result of some unusual or abnormal process, such as nervous biting habits or faulty tooth-brushing methods.

Abscess: A localized collection of pus.

Abutment: Natural tooth to which one end of a fixed or removable partial denture is attached.

Acute: Having a rapid onset, showing pronounced symptoms, and lasting a relatively short time; not chronic.

Ala: The wing of the nostril.

Allergy: Hypersensitivity to some substance.

Alloy: A mixture of two or more metals that are mutually soluble in the molten condition.

Alveolar: Pertaining to the processes of the jaws in which the roots of the teeth are embedded.

Alveolus: The cavity or socket in the alveolar process in which the roots of a tooth are held by the periodontal ligament.

Amalgam: An alloy of silver, tin, copper, and zinc mixed with mercury.

Ameloblast: Enamel-forming cell.

Ampule: A small glass container that, when sealed, holds solutions or other preparations under sterile conditions.

Analgesic: An agent used to relieve pain.

Anaphylactic Shock: A severe allergic reaction.

Anesthesia: Loss of sensation.

Anesthetic: An agent that causes anesthesia.

Anterior Teeth: Teeth located in the front of the mouth: the incisors and cuspids.

Antibiotic: A chemical substance produced by certain microorganisms that will inhibit the growth of or destroy other microorganisms.

Antidote: A remedy for counteracting the effects of a poison.

Antiseptic: An agent that prevents or arrests the growth of microorganisms without destroying them.

Antisialagogue: An agent that checks the flow of the saliva.

Apex: Tip or end of a tooth root.

Apical: Pertaining to the apex.

Apicoectomy: Cutting off the apex of a tooth root; root resection.

Aspiration: The act of breathing or drawing in; the act of removing fluids from a cavity by means of a suction device.

Attrition: The normal wearing away of the tooth surfaces.

Autoclave: An apparatus that sterilizes instruments and materials by subjecting them to steam under pressure.

Bacterial Plaque: Colorless, jelly-like deposit that clings to the surface of a tooth; it is made up primarily of bacteria, cells, and sticky substances from the saliva.

Bactericide: An agent that destroys bacteria.

Bacteriostatic: Inhibiting the growth and reproduction of bacteria.

Bacterium: Any one of a large class of microorganisms.

Bevel: A slanting edge or surface.

Blood Pressure: The force exerted by the blood against the walls of the arteries.

Bone: The hard, rigid connective tissue; the hardest substance in the body except for enamel and dentin. A part of the skeleton, such as the sternum (breastbone) or the maxilla.

Buccal: Pertaining to the cheek; sometimes used to refer to the outer surface of a posterior tooth.

Calcification: The hardening of organic tissue because of deposits of calcium salts within the tissue.

Calculus: Calcified material adhering to the tooth surface either above the gingiva (supragingival calculus) or below the gingiva (subgingival calculus).

Capillary: Any of the minute, hair-like vessels connecting arteries and veins.

Cardiopulmonary Resuscitation (CPR): The combination of external cardiac compressions with artificial ventilation to revive a victim of cardiac arrest.

Caries: Decay of tooth structure.

Carpule: Trademark for a glass cartridge containing anesthetic solution, which is loaded into a syringe.

Cellulitis: Inflammation of cellular tissue.

Cementum: A bone-like substance that covers the tooth root and assists in supporting the tooth.

Cervical Line: A slight indentation that encircles a tooth, marking the junction of the crown with the root.

Chronic: Persisting over a long period of time; not acute.

Cingulum: A lingual elevation or lobe located within the cervical third of an anterior tooth.

Coagulation: The process by which blood changes from a fluid into a clot.

Congenital: Existing at birth.

Connective Tissue: The binding and supporting tissue of the body, such as bone, cartilage, and ligaments.

Contagious: Capable of being transmitted by contact from one person to another.

Contamination: The introduction of impurities or disease-producing organisms.

Contraction: The shortening, as of a muscle, in response to a stimulus.

Convulsion: Violent, involuntary contraction of the voluntary muscles.

Crown: The top part of a tooth. The anatomic crown is the part of the tooth covered with enamel. The clinical crown is the part of the tooth that is exposed (visible) in the mouth.

Cusp: A round or conical point on or near the working surface of a cuspid, bicuspid, or molar.

Cyanosis: Blueness of the skin, especially the area around the mouth and under the fingernails, due to lack of oxygen in the blood.

Cyst: A sac that contains liquid or semisolid material; usually an abnormal process.

Debridement: Surgical removal of foreign matter and damaged or infected tissue from a wound.

Deciduous: Not permanent; used to designate the teeth of the first dentition (the "baby teeth").

Dental Health Team: A team of two or more members—the dental officer, the dental assistant, and others—whose purpose is to serve the military community by caring for its dental health needs.

Dentin: That substance making up the bulk of the tooth. Primary dentin is formed before the tooth erupts; secondary dentin is formed after tooth eruption to protect the pulp from irritation.

Dentinoenamel Junction: The point at which the dentin and enamel meet.

Dentition: The natural teeth.

Diagnosis: The art of determining the nature of a disease.

Disease: Any departure from a state of health.

Disinfectant: An agent that destroys disease-producing microorganisms.

Distal: Away from the midline; the surface of a tooth that, following the curvature of the dental arch, faces away from the midline.

Edema: Swelling due to the collection of fluid in tissues.

Enamel: The hardest tissue of the body; it covers and protects the coronal portion of the dentin.

Enamel Hyoplasia: Defective or incomplete development of enamel.

Epiglottis: The lid-like structure that covers the entrance to the larynx.

Epithelial Attachment: The attachment of the gingiva to the tooth by means of epithelium.

Erosion: Wearing away or loss of tooth structure, usually resulting in smooth, shallow, V-like depressions.

Exudate: Fluid, cells, or cellular debris present in tissues or on tissue surfaces, usually as a result of inflammation or trauma.

Facial: Pertaining to the face; the outer (buccal and labial) surfaces of the teeth.

Fissure: A cleft or groove in the enamel on the occlusal surface of a tooth resulting from the imperfect union of cusp margins.

Foramen: A hole in a bone of the body that permits the passage of nerves and blood vessels.

Fossa: A shallow depression in the surface of a tooth.

Germicide: An agent that destroys bacteria.

Gingiva: The soft tissue covering the alveolar processes and encircling the necks of the teeth.

Gingivitis: Inflammation of the gingival tissue.

Groove: A linear depression in the surface of a tooth.

Hemorrhage: Bleeding.

Hemostat: An instrument or drug used to stop bleeding.

Horizontal Overlap: A condition in which the horizontal distance between the maxillary and mandibular incisal edges is abnormal when the other teeth are in normal occlusion. Also called overjet or "buck teeth."

Incisal Edge: The cutting edge of an anterior tooth.

Infection: Invasion of the tissues of the body by microorganisms in such a way as to favor their growth and development and permit their toxins to injure the tissues.

Inflammation: The reaction of tissue to irritation or injury, usually characterized by pain, heat, redness, and swelling.

Inlay: A restoration made outside the mouth and cemented into a prepared cavity.

Interproximal Space: The space between contacting (adjoining) teeth gingival to the contact area.

Labial: Pertaining to the lip; the outer (facial) surface of an anterior tooth.

Lateral: Toward the side or away from the midline.

Lesion: A change in structure or function of a tissue or part of the body due to injury or disease.

Line Angle: A line or angle formed by the junction of two surfaces of a tooth.

Lingual: Pertaining to the tongue; the surface of an anterior or posterior tooth that is toward the tongue.

Malocclusion: Any deviation from normal occlusion.

Mandible: The bone that forms the lower jaw.

Margin: The edge formed by joining together two surfaces, such as the distal and occlusal surfaces of posterior teeth.

Mastication: Chewing.

Maxillae: The two facial bones that unite to form the upper jaw.

Medial: Pertaining to the middle.

Median: Situated in the middle.

Membrane: A thin layer of tissue.

Mesial: Toward the midline; the surface of a tooth that, following the curvature of the dental arch, faces toward the midline.

Microorganism: A microscopically small living organism.

Mucosa: A mucous membrane, such as the lining of the oral cavity.

Necrosis: Death of a cell, or of a group of cells, in contact with living tissue.

Necrotic: Pertaining to or affected with necrosis.

Necrotizing Ulcerative Gingivitis (NUG): Severe inflammation of the gingival tissue.

Oblique Ridge: A ridge on the occlusal surface of a maxillary molar.

Occlusal: Pertaining to the chewing surfaces of posterior teeth.

Occlusion: The relationship between the occlusal surfaces of opposing maxillary and mandibular teeth when the teeth are in contact.

Odontoblast: Dentin-forming cell.

Osseous: Bony.

Palatal: Referring to the palate or roof of the mouth.

Palate: The roof of the mouth.

Papilla: Gingival tissue filling the interproximal space.

Pericoronitis: An inflammation of the gingiva around the crown of a partially erupted tooth.

Periodontal Abscess: An abscess caused by infection in the periodontium.

Periodontal Disease: A broad term for a number of diseases that affect the periodontium.

Periodontal Ligament: Fibrous tissue that surrounds a tooth root and attaches the root to its bony socket.

Periodontal Pocket: A gingival sulcus that has increased in depth because of periodontal disease.

Periodontitis: Inflammation of the periodontium.

Periodontium: The tissues that surround and support the teeth: the cementum, the alveolar process, the periodontal ligament, and the gingiva.

Pharmacology: The science dealing with the study of the action of drugs on living systems.

Point Angle: A point or angle formed by the junction of three surfaces of a tooth.

Posterior Teeth: Teeth located in the back of the mouth: the bicuspids and the molars.

Prescribe: To designate, recommend, or order a remedy or treatment.

Prescription: Written instructions for preparing and administering a remedy.

Pulp: The soft tissue that normally fills the pulp cavity. It contains nerve and blood vessels, maintains the vitality of the tooth, and forms dentin. Also referred to as the dental pulp.

Pus: A thick fluid formed in connection with inflammation.

Radiography: Recording images of a patient's internal structures on film by using X-rays.

Radiolucent: Permitting the passage of X-rays or other forms of radiation; refers to structures that appear dark on radiographs.

Radiopaque: Not permitting the passage of X-rays or other forms of radiation; refers to structures that appear light on radiographs.

Respiration: The act of breathing.

Restoration: The replacement of missing tooth structure; a material or device used for this purpose.

Resuscitation: The act of reviving a person who is unconscious or who appears to be dead.

Ridge: A linear elevation on a tooth.

Root Canal: Hollow, usually tubular, portion of the tooth root that extends from the pulp chamber to the apical foramen and serves as a passageway for nerves and blood vessels.

Sedative: An agent that allays apprehension, irritability, or excitement.

Shock: Acute circulatory failure due to inadequate volume of circulating blood, brought about by physical or emotional trauma.

Sterile: Free from living microorganisms.

Stomatitis: A general term used to denote inflammation of the oral mucosa.

Subcutaneous: Under the skin.

Supernumerary: Extra; more than the normal number.

Temporomandibular Joint (TMJ): The joint formed by the condyle of the mandible and the glenoid fossa of the temporal bone.

Therapy: Treatment.

Topical: Pertaining to the surface.

Trachea: The windpipe.

Tragus: A projection of cartilage located in front of the external opening of the ear.

Tranquilizer: An agent that induces calmness.

Transverse Ridge: A ridge on the occlusal surface of a tooth formed by the junction of the facial and lingual triangular ridges.

Trauma: Injury or wound.

Triangular Ridge: A ridge on the occlusal surface of a tooth that slopes down from the tip of a cusp toward the center of the occlusal surface.

Trituration: The process of mixing mercury with a metal alloy to produce a plastic mass suitable for use in restoring teeth.

Ulcer: An open sore on the skin or mucous membrane.

Unconscious: Insensible; unaware of self or environment.

Vertical Overlap: A condition in which the vertical distance between the maxillary and mandibular incisal edges is abnormal when the other teeth are in normal occlusion. Also called overbite.

Wisdom Tooth: A term used for the third molar.